Tiny Blue LINES

"How easy it is to forget that at the center of the Christian story is a woman in an unplanned pregnancy. Chaunie Brusie reveals how she was not alone in her own turbulent transition to motherhood—how God holds each life precious and lights the way forward. *Tiny Blue Lines* is a triumph of faith and courage, and a treasury of resources for all who choose life."

Margaret H. Hartshorn
President, Heartbeat International

"*Tiny Blue Lines* is the perfect choice for that young woman facing an unexpected pregnancy. Chaunie Brusie's brave telling of her own story opens the doors for other young women to be honest with themselves and their situations. Throughout this book, you will be guided through Brusie's experience, as well as be introduced to many young moms who have been through this. While those tiny blue lines mark the end of one journey, they introduce a new beginning—full of new experiences and opportunities! *Tiny Blue Lines* reminds mothers that they are strong enough to embrace the challenges and welcome the joys of young motherhood. This book will provide great encouragement for any young woman as she courageously pursues this new life."

Kristan Hawkins
President, Students for Life of America

"You'll find yourself changed and improved by the journey you'll take with Chaunie Brusie in *Tiny Blue Lines*. Buckle up, saddle up, and get ready: you'll laugh, you'll cry, you'll be close to rolling on the floor. It will not only impact your worldview, it will give you hope and encouragement in equal measure."

Sarah Reinhard
Author of *A Catholic Mother's Companion to Pregnancy*

Tiny Blue LINES

Reclaiming Your Life, Preparing for
Your Baby, and Moving Forward with
Faith in an Unplanned Pregnancy

Chaunie Marie Brusie

ave maria press AmP notre dame, indiana

Founded in 1865, Ave Maria Press is a ministry of the United States Province of Holy Cross.

www.avemariapress.com

Paperback: ISBN-13 978-1-59471-424-5

E-book: ISBN-13 978-1-59471-425-2

Cover and text design by Andy Wagoner.

Printed and bound in the United States of America.

Library of Congress Cataloging-in-Publication Data is available.

For my family

Contents

Additional Resources

Foreword

Throughout my adult life, I have been more than a little familiar with the unwed mom phenomenon, usually via a barrage of statistics and government reports. Occasionally, I've had the chance to have a long chat with a woman, now long into her childrearing years, who can reflect back on what it was like to have her first child while single. *Tiny Blue Lines*, on the other hand, places me and you right smack in the middle of the "event" as it is unfolding today, in our own towns, our own colleges, and even in our own churches.

Tiny Blue Lines puts you not only on the scene, but in it. If you're a mother, you can imagine yourself on the telephone taking the call from your daughter. If you're the best friend, or the boyfriend, the college administrator or the health center nurse, the nosy shopper or the well-meaning parishioner, you can better understand why the first thing that flies into your head may not be the thing that should fly out of your mouth.

But more than this, if you are that girl or that woman . . . the scared, pregnant one . . . you need the humor, the stories, the practical advice, the perspective that this graced little book so generously provides. Every woman on earth is overcome in a real way when she first learns that she is no longer alone because she is "with child." The single woman is more so. How do we tell her that her life is not over but in so many, many ways, just begun? We can try, especially we mothers who know that we always get more life than we give. But the bilingual gifts of Chaunie Marie Brusie are better suited to the task. She speaks "girl" and "woman." What a gift to every young mother and her child!

Helen M. Alvaré
Author of *Breaking Through*

Introduction

As you may have already figured out, I had an unplanned pregnancy during my senior year of college. I was completely shocked, unprepared, and ill-equipped to bring a baby into this world when the two tiny blue lines appeared on my drugstore pregnancy test. Chances are, if you're holding this book, you're in a similar situation and feeling just as terrified as I did.

I needed help facing my pregnancy, but I didn't know where to turn for that help. After all, I wasn't a helpless teenager; I was a senior in college. I had a long-term boyfriend *and* a full-tuition scholarship to college. I was a motivated, intelligent, and capable woman. And, as many people were quick to tell me, I should have known better.

There seemed to be a lot of help and support for teenage pregnancies, even older pregnancies, but for women like me—the in-between, the not-too-young, and yet not-too-old—everything was a blur.

I sought desperately to find others like me out there. I didn't fit in with the older soccer mom crowd, and I wasn't exactly teenage mom material, either. As an independent young woman in college, my needs and experiences were different. But I couldn't find anything relating to women like me. The unspoken consensus surrounding unplanned pregnancy for college-age women seemed to be that we should just deal with it—or get rid of it.

I needed help navigating my new life. Since the information and support for moms like me were lacking, I decided to create my own support network. Through my story, and the stories of so many other mothers like me, I hope you will learn that you are not alone, that there is no "right" way to get through a planned or unplanned pregnancy as a young mom. Most of all, I want you to know that you *can* succeed as a mother, as a student, and as a professional. By surrounding myself with strong and amazing moms, I made it, and I know you can, too—hopefully *without* the massive display of stretch marks that I have managed to accumulate.

Through this book, I want to share the advice of all the amazing mothers who have helped and inspired me. By the time you read this book, I will be twenty-seven with three young children, so I've gained a few notches on my young-mom belt. (I'm still working on losing the baby weight, okay?) You'll also find straight talk from women like me who have been there for it all: telling our parents, figuring out final exams, and giving birth. You'll laugh, you'll cry, you'll probably take a couple of bathroom breaks, but most important, you will discover that you are not alone.

So break out the maternity pants, sister—we have a long nine months ahead of us!

CHAPTER ONE

What If I'm Pregnant?

It's the question that women in every century, in every part of the world have asked.

What if I'm pregnant?

The question lingered in the back of my mind one day on a weekend home from college. Ben, my boyfriend of four years, my siblings, and I had stopped by the grocery store and picked up food for a picnic in the park on a gorgeous fall afternoon. *It's just a normal Sunday*, I tried to convince myself. *Everything will be fine.*

I took a bite of my pumpkin-spice doughnut and tried to nibble on my favorite chips, but I couldn't hide the waves of nausea I was fighting. It wasn't long before I clutched my stomach in agony and curled up in the fetal position on our musty yellow picnic blanket.

"What's wrong with you?" Ben asked me.

I laughed it off, chalking my upset stomach up to the junk food. "I just ate too much. I'm sure that's all it is."

But later that evening, at my parents' house, I spent most of the time lying on the couch, unable to shake my nausea or the desire to sleep for a thousand years.

That night, Ben and I headed back to school. As we drove, I hesitantly turned to Ben and told him that my period was a little late.

"How late?" he asked.

I felt the blood drain from my face. "Um, well, it's just a little late. . . . Let me think. I had it in August, so it's only . . . three weeks late."

"But I'm sure I'm getting it today," I rushed on, "I'm sure that's why I feel so awful."

Ben continued driving in silence, his face emotionless.

What if . . . ?

That night, I decided to take a pregnancy test.

"There's no way I'm pregnant," I said to Ben as we stood in my kitchen, trying and failing to keep my voice from rising in panic. "But I'm sick of worrying about it. I'll just take the test, and that will be the end of it."

And so I found myself sitting anxiously in the passenger seat and chugging a water bottle as Ben sped to the store at 2:00 a.m. We left the first store after discovering that they kept their pregnancy tests locked up. There was no way I could actually bring myself to admit *out loud* that I needed a pregnancy test. *Ridiculous!* I thought, *when I'm obviously not even pregnant!*

Finally, we ended up at a Rite Aid. I browsed the selection of pregnancy tests while Ben pretended to examine batteries in the next aisle. The choices were overwhelming. Should I get the e.p.t® or chance the off-brand? Did I want one test, or two?

Finally, after staring at the tests for what felt like hours, I grabbed a box of two tests and headed toward the register. As we checked out, I found myself staring at the young cashier, memorizing a face I knew I would never forget and wondering how he could possibly ring us up so calmly when my life could be changing forever.

When I got home, I attempted to read the instructions and realized I was having trouble deciphering the words because my hands were shaking. That ruled out the whole peeing-on-the-stick thing, so I did my duty and carried the cup to the kitchen, where Ben sat waiting in the corner. I held the test poised over the edge of the cup for a minute, hoping and praying that I could prevent my life from crashing around me for just a moment longer.

I held my breath and dipped the test.

What if . . . ?

Before the test was even fully submerged, I saw it.

Two tiny blue lines innocently aligned in the form of a presumptuous "plus" sign.

I screamed. I tore open the second pregnancy test and dunked it. Positive again. I stared down at those two tiny blue lines, illuminated by the fluorescent light of my student apartment, with my boyfriend motionless in the corner, and I screamed, a sound that felt like it couldn't possibly be coming from me.

I was twenty-one, unmarried, a student in my senior year of college, and still taking my laundry home to my parents every weekend.

The question of "What if I'm pregnant?" quickly became "What the heck am I going to do now?"

CHAPTER TWO

What Now? Your Future as a Young Mom

~~~~~~

Three weeks before I took my pregnancy test, Ben and I sat doing homework at a coffee shop near campus.

"So, what do you think about getting married while we're in Italy?" I asked Ben casually.

He raised one eyebrow at me over the stack of books that crowded our table.

"Just imagine it—a beautiful white dress, the ancient church, a romantic gondola ride—what do you think?" I continued, growing more excited by my flash of inspiration.

Ben just shook his blond head at me and sipped his double-chocolate-chip Frappuccino®.

Senior year of college was going great. I had just finished an awesome internship in Washington, DC, found my first "real" apartment, and my boyfriend and I were planning to study abroad in Italy for the next semester. I had high hopes for a relaxing senior year filled with good friends, fun times, and a few drinks to celebrate my newly acquired legal drinking status. (Oh, the irony.)

Yes, ma'am. I had a lot of high hopes and dreams—none of which included having a baby during my senior year of college.

When I found out I was pregnant, I'll be honest with you—my first thoughts weren't about the baby. They were about *me*. Many women, myself included, worry about how having a baby at a young age will affect their life plans. Not only do they fear disappointing their parents, being left out by their peers, and being stigmatized as unwed mothers, but they also fear losing the lives they once dreamed of.

"Before I found out I was pregnant, I was a good student," Jessica Watson, a mother of four, writes. "I had plans to go to college and possibly law school."

Kayla McAfee was twenty-three years old and living with her sister in Germany, working a "crappy resort job" in order to travel when she began experiencing terrible morning sickness. Kayla writes,

When I finally admitted to myself that something was off, I bought a pregnancy test at a German drugstore. My first attempt at the test was on a train because I was too impatient to wait the hour and a half until we got home. I couldn't read the instructions (they were in German) but I knew the basics of how pregnancy tests work, so I peed on the stick, waited the appropriate amount of time and crossed my fingers for one line. Nothing showed up. I waited a little while longer and then hid the test in my purse and took it to my seat to show my sister. Apparently I'm an idiot, since I peed on the protective covering, not the actual stick.

The second attempt took place in a dorm bathroom. I locked the door, and this time I peed in a cup and then stuck the (unwrapped) test into it. Fully prepared to wait the three minutes, within thirty seconds there were two very distinct lines. My immediate reaction was panic. All my plans, dreams, and goals for the future instantly flashed through my mind, my stomach dropped, my eyes welled with tears, and I cursed, repeatedly, a long string of expletives.

Accepting my pregnancy was difficult. I had a list of places I had yet to visit and plans to move to Chicago and attend acting school. When I pictured kids, I envisioned myself as at least thirty years old with a kick-ass artistic career, a comfortable bank account, and a guy that loved me and would love my kids. And here I was, three days from twenty-four, unmarried, broke, working a minimum-wage job and about to become a single mom.

Mandy Lange, a twenty-two-year-old mother and future teacher, says,

All of my life I had been trying to plan, to reach goals, and most importantly, be someone my family was proud of. In that moment, when I discovered I was blessed with a child, I felt as far from my image of perfection as I ever had. I could not move. I could not think of my child. I could only mourn the loss of my old self, the person I had been just that morning. It was the first time in my adult life that I had no idea of how to proceed. That feeling of helplessness, of not knowing what would come, was pretty new to my organized, privileged life.

Raquel Kato, a twenty-one-year-old Catholic senior on her college basketball team, found out she was pregnant just as she was preparing for grad school. "I wish that I could tell you this awesome, inspiring story of how optimistic I was when I found out I was pregnant and how well I handled the adversity, but my reaction was not pretty. I felt horror. Panic. Denial. Absolute shock. Embarrassment. Shame. Just to name a few," says Raquel. "At that moment in my life I felt like I was trapped in complete darkness, like I was suffocating and I was alone. I had a lot going for me. I had big dreams and plans, but having a baby out of wedlock was *not* a part of that plan."

Meagan Francis, one my idols in life (she's a mom of five *and* an amazing writer!), became pregnant at age nineteen with her boyfriend. "I thought my life was pretty much over," says Meagan about her pregnancy.

> While there were many terrifying things about being pregnant at the age of twenty-one, to my goal-driven and ambitious self, the fear that I wouldn't amount to anything ranked the highest on my list. On top of that fear, it was hard to wrap my mind around the fact that I had entered into motherhood in a way that, truth be told, I wasn't really proud of. I worried that if I couldn't even get the pregnancy part right, how would I figure the rest of my life out?
>
> I dreamed of traveling the world, working for a woman's advocacy non-profit, becoming a writer, going to graduate school, and starting my own business. But when I got pregnant, I not only feared that none of that would happen; I also didn't feel worthy of trying to make it happen. I felt like somehow my "bad start" to motherhood meant my entire life track would be thrown out of whack. Like I had set the train off motion and wouldn't ever be able to fix it. In my twisted sense of grief, I thought I somehow deserved a tougher time of it all, because that's what happens when you're not married and pregnant, right? You're supposed to struggle.
>
> Well, I'm here to tell you now . . .
> Don't believe it.

As I did, and many other surprise moms have come to find out, having a baby does not ruin your plans, but in many cases, actually helps you achieve the goals that matter the most to you.

For example, I have always wanted to be a writer. I sailed through high school English classes and had scribbled praises from my teacher in the margins of my papers during the sole writing class I took during college. I was always good at writing and enjoyed it but had never even considered studying writing as a possible career. Instead, I focused on pursuing a career in health care—because the best students go into medicine, right? I couldn't fathom the thought of medical school, so I chose nursing, with my sights set on working in labor and delivery. I wound up hating nursing and contemplated switching my major more times than I can count, but I continued on, because again, that's what good students do, right?

Then, after I became pregnant with Ada, I started writing about the difficulties I had uncovered for pregnant students at my college. That led to a work-at-home job for the nonprofit organization Feminists for Life, which led to traveling and speaking about my story. That job made me realize how great working at home was with a family, which led me to start thinking about a real career as a writer. Throw in a few more kids and even more time at home, and the thinking about writing turned into a blog and then, remarkably, this book.

Can you see where I'm going with this?

Becoming pregnant at the age of twenty-one didn't ruin my plans. In fact, it actually helped, in a completely Walt Disney way, to make all my dreams come true.

And truth be told, I'm not the only young mom who has had that experience. Over and over, the moms I have talked to say that having a baby at a youngish age helped them to either get their lives in order or reprioritize their goals and focus on creating new lives for themselves.

Young-mom Kim explained how having her daughter prompted her to further her own education. "I do have a greater ambition to go back to school," Kim told me. "I never really did before, but I want my daughter to be able to have whatever she wants. I want her to know that I've worked for her. My dream is to graduate from college and get a good career to raise a beautiful, intelligent daughter and build a beautiful house for us. I know this will happen, too, because I'm going to do it for her."

As my writing idol Meagan Francis says, "I was basically floundering through life until I had kids—it grounded me, brought my priorities into clear focus, and gave me the impetus to do the things I wanted to do."

Another writing great and young mommy extraordinaire, Tara Pringle Jefferson of *The Young Mommy Life* blog says, "Motherhood essentially gave me my career. I didn't realize what I wanted to do with my life (help young mothers succeed) until I became one myself. Life does not often follow a linear path."

Penelope Trunk, a bestselling author and career advisor for businesses and women, wrote an intriguing article that encouraged women looking for careers to have kids early on in life, rather than later.

Her reasoning? It's just easier. It's so much easier for women to have babies while they are young and then ease into their careers, rather than go full-force into their careers and then try to have babies. It's fighting biology, for one thing, but it's also facing the fact that motherhood, no matter what, does create some waves in your life. We can talk about women having it all until we are blue in the face, but that still doesn't change the fact that having babies takes work.

Women give birth to their babies, and someone needs to feed and change them. It's just plain harder to do that in the midst of building a career. It's not impossible, of course. But Penelope pointed out that maybe instead of encouraging women to build up amazing careers, then take time off to have kids and try to continue doing both, we should encourage women looking to have careers and motherhood to have babies first, at a "young" age, and then be a little more free—both in time and mental energy—to build up a career later on, if that's what they choose.

So, did you get all that? We're doing things the right way! Heck, some women in high-powered careers may even (gasp) envy us! Fifty is the new forty and forty is the new twenty, so at this rate, we will be in our twenties forever. Plus, let's not too lightly look on the fact that it has to be a lot easier to bounce back in the body department if we're having kids now. Okay, so that's not exactly been the case for me, but someone has to keep the yoga-pants style going strong.

It's really important to have the conversation that an unplanned pregnancy at a young age is *not* a dead end. There is a huge disparity among women in their early twenties who become pregnant and those who stay pregnant. When I first started writing this book, the statistics showed that one million women aged twenty to twenty-nine became unexpectedly pregnant in the United States each year. Surprisingly, as I wrote this book, the numbers just continue to grow. At last count, more than 1.3 million women in their twenties become unexpectedly pregnant in the United States each year alone. And women between the ages of twenty-two and twenty-four have the highest number of unplanned pregnancies. The one thing that hasn't changed, however, is the outcome of the pregnancies. Consistently, the majority of unintended pregnancies to women in their twenties end in abortion.[†]

---

† http://www.thenationalcampaign.org/resources/pdf/briefly-unplanned-pregnancy-among-unmarried.pdf

I find that fact troubling. I bring this up not out of a desire to start a rousing political debate or get you all fired up about choice, but because I can't help but wonder what that tells us about young motherhood. In 2008, there were 6.6 million pregnancies in women of all ages and more than *half* of those were unplanned. Clearly, unplanned pregnancy is not a rare occurrence, but for women our age? Unplanned pregnancies represent a lot more than just surprise babies—they represent the end of our lives as we know them.

The early twenties are such a critical time in our lives—or at least that's what we're told, right? That it's the time in our lives to be selfish and to figure out what we want to do, dance naked in the rain, and learn it all and do it all before we settle down and lose all our sense of adventure and fun when we have families. In some ways, an unplanned pregnancy in your early twenties can feel more shameful than a teenage pregnancy. We're not "careless" and irresponsible teens who didn't know any better. We're educated, motivated adults destined to do great things, so the fact that we "let" ourselves get pregnant doesn't seem to fit with the picture. I'll never forget during my first pregnancy when I was having lunch one day with an older woman that I worked with occasionally. Seated in the booth across from me, she shook her head at me over her chopped salad and chided gently, "I just don't understand how, in this day and age, with all the birth control options out there, *women let themselves get pregnant.*" As writer Michelle Horton commented in an article featured on CNN.com, "Are twenty-something unwed moms the new teen moms? If referring to how both groups of mothers are treated and shamed, then yes: we are the new teen moms."

Everyone is pretty quick to blame the woman for getting pregnant. And yes, we made the choice to have sex, but we're obviously not alone there. And yes, I wholeheartedly support the idea that sex is designed for marriage and that marriage is a built-in protector against all of the struggles that a pregnancy outside of wedlock can bring, but I also know that unplanned pregnancy happens. Even for non-Catholic couples who use birth control, unplanned pregnancy happens. You've seen *Jurassic Park*, right? Nature always finds a way—it's necessary to our whole survival as a human race. With the advent of "family planning," in fact, there almost seems to be *more* pressure to have the perfect life put together before having kids as a young adult.

For young mothers in their early twenties, that positive pregnancy test also brings out the fear that we won't be able to figure out who we are as women before we become mothers. We won't get the chance to finish school, pursue our dream jobs, or travel the world, because we'll be tied down with kids.

And while I will say that having kids does make some things more difficult, I do refuse to say that having children early ruins our lives. All around me, young mothers are creating their own paths and finishing college, going on to graduate school, living inspiring and beautiful lives while refusing to accept that young motherhood is a dead end. "When you have an unplanned pregnancy, your dreams don't fail; they change," said my friend Lauren Furneaux. "You just have someone there cheering you on and joining your journey to your dreams coming true."

So in a way, I see abortion as a somewhat failed message on behalf of our fellow young mothers. I have to wonder if that high rate of abortion among women our age sends the message that *we can't do this.* Because if the majority of us choose abortion, who do we have as an example of what a successful life as a young mother looks like? And who do we have standing next to us, showing the world that young motherhood is worth doing?

I won't lie when I tell you that abortion absolutely crossed my mind. Even though I grew up with pro-life beliefs, the thought of an abortion popped up in my mind almost as soon as those two blue lines did. Nothing about pregnancy in those first few weeks felt real. I didn't really feel that different, and I couldn't fathom how there could actually be a human being growing inside me. (This is still kind of hard to believe. Three people have come from my body. *What?*)

The thought that something could help me rewind time was so, so tempting. All I really wanted in that time after I found out I was pregnant was to make everything go back to normal. Abortion sounded tempting, primarily because I was scared. I was scared that I wouldn't be a good mother. Scared that I would always be seen as "that girl who got pregnant." Scared that my marriage would be over before it had even really started. Scared that I wouldn't amount to anything after this. Scared that my family would hate me forever.

But there was also a part of me that rebelled against the idea of abortion. It felt like choosing abortion would be admitting that I couldn't do this, that I shouldn't do this, or that somehow, my baby and I didn't deserve this.

Abortion, in a way, felt like selling myself short.

While I know that every situation is different, but with every abortion, are we sending the message that motherhood is a dead end? That combining motherhood and selfhood—and even young womanhood—can't be done?

I know the arguments for abortion. As a nurse, I've seen a lot of the hard cases. I've seen a thirteen-year-old girl raped and impregnated by her own father; I've seen a mother collapse in tears when her baby was given a terminal diagnosis before he'd even had a chance to live outside her womb; I've seen a woman beaten and bruised by her husband just for getting pregnant again.

I've seen them and cried for them and wondered what was best for them. We think of abortion because we want to help these women. We want to end their suffering, and we are afraid of adding the task of caring for a baby to their plight. I get that. I really, really do.

But I also hate to see us limit ourselves as women. Maybe it's just me, but I hate to be told that I *can't* do something. That it will be too hard, or that it will inconvenience the precious world of men.

To me, abortion, in a way, is telling that young girl that she is too broken to repair. To me, abortion is telling that mother that her baby, flawed already, isn't worth the fight. To me, abortion is telling that woman that her husband is right—that she and her baby are nuisances.

One of my best friends had a huge fight with her boyfriend when they found out that she was unexpectedly expecting. "We had a trip planned to an amusement park," Megan recalled. "I was a week late and took a test before we left—it was a digital and read 'inconclusive.' For the first time in my life, I got sick on rides, and got a migraine the last day. We had to leave early, and I almost threw up because I was so hungry—I knew something was wrong. I took another test about a week later, on a Saturday before I got in the shower. This time, it was one of those two-lines tests—two blue lines. I cried in the shower," Megan told me.

Later, her boyfriend brought up abortion. "The one thing he said was, "What would this to do us if we go through with this pregnancy?" Megan recalls. "And I said, '*What will this do to me if we don't?*'"

Megan's words are so profound to me, because I feel that, all debates aside, they force us to consider what kind of message it sends when sixty-five thousand women our age are choosing abortion every year. Are those women choosing abortion as a free and empowered choice? Because without positive role models and other women showing us that it is possible, how can we know that those two tiny blue lines aren't a straight shot to a dead-end road?

I want young women and mothers to feel empowered. I want us to feel empowered in the choice to become mothers and empowered to continue to carve out our lives as women—both personally and professionally. And I believe that starts with women sharing their stories, both failures and triumphs. Because it's not helpful to say that motherhood is all rainbows and butterflies and having a baby is "just the best thing ever."

Like anything else in life, there are good days and bad days with young motherhood. It can be really challenging, especially if you don't have a supportive partner. I will tell you honestly that I have been so tired that I have yelled at my poor, crying baby and called my mother in desperation, because I was so exhausted that I couldn't see straight. But then I will tell you that I have also been reduced to tears of joy in the grocery store parking lot, just watching my daughter catch snowflakes on her tongue and getting lost in the sheer happiness of loving her.

Regardless of how you feel about the abortion issue, I think we can all agree that creating more positive role models of young motherhood is a good thing. And those young mothers (um, you?) will go on to change society and the workplace to accommodate a world that is okay with families and babies, which is also a good thing. Then, more young women will realize that they *can* do this motherhood thing when their surprise two lines show up, and they will go on to have awesome kids that will go on to create a better world, and so on and so forth, until we're all standing around in a circle, holding hands and singing with pure, unadulterated, young-mommyhood joy.

I want to celebrate young mothers, not because we are young, but because we are just darn good mothers and people. We aren't afraid to make our own paths, continue our educations, stay home with our babies, work, or pursue our passions. I want to celebrate our strengths while not asking to be seen as anything less than any other mom. I try to be a realist. I've had to work harder and longer at my goals. But, I'm still working at them!

I browsed through a book titled *Mission Adulthood: How The Twenty-somethings of Today are Transforming Work, Love, and Life* the other day, contemplating if I wanted to purchase it. In the book's introduction, the author discussed how he specifically chose twenty-somethings to study who "hadn't short-circuited their life goals by starting families early . . ." (p. 11).

As soon as I read those words, I slammed the book shut. Because I don't buy into the fact that having a family early means "short-circuiting" my life goals. I also didn't buy that book. *Hmmpph.* I like to think that by surrounding myself with positive role models—women who have chosen young motherhood and have worked to see it as an empowering choice—that I am part of a group of women who can change the world by incorporating our families into pursuing our life goals.

Emily of the blog *Your Mom Goes to College* is an inspiring young mother who was recently diagnosed with cancer. She pretty much stole my heart for the best fist-pumping young-mom inspiration ever when she said, "My son does not hold me back from being the person I want to be; he does not inhibit my life in any way. I know that the things I dream of doing are within my grasp, not despite the fact that I have a four-year-old . . . but *because* I do." Oh, and this: "Never underestimate the power of a child's love and the strength of a mother. You *can* do anything you want if you are willing to put forth the effort."

In looking back on her surprise pregnancy, writer and young-mom Michelle Horton says, "I wish I knew that things were going to fall into place. That all of the stress wasn't worth it. Because while I was focused on how my life would change, I didn't know that the biggest surprise would be that the life I knew, that I was desperately clinging to, wouldn't matter to me. I would have new values, new emotions, new priorities—and I would become exactly who I was always meant to be."

I also really like Darlene's honest attitude about young mother-hood. She writes a blog called *Tales of a Young Momma*. After having two children, Darlene put her education on hold. "School is very far down the line of my priority list right now, and at first I was ashamed to admit that. I had been so school- and career-driven that I forced myself to continue when [my son] Jasper was young. Not because it was as important to me, but because I was afraid others would see me as a failure," says Darlene. "I was afraid they would say having a baby ruined my future and plans."

I think it's so important to mention this point, because while I'm all very *rah-rah* and *young moms can take over the world*, the truth is, sometimes having kids does change our priorities, goals, and dreams. And changing your goals to include motherhood does not equate failure.

"I finally started to see that it's okay to admit that goals change," explains Darlene. "I no longer dream of being a kick-ass attorney like I used to; now I dream of library trips and baking with my children, and traveling with them whenever possible to show them the world, and I think that's okay as well. Becoming a mom wasn't me settling or giving up my goals and dreams; it became my new dream after Jasper was born."

The bottom line is, don't lose sight of who you are just because you are a mother. Don't sell yourself short. You may need to do a little reconfiguring to get there, but you can combine selfhood and motherhood. It will take constant recalibration, but don't be afraid of it. And in fact, I happen to think that working on your personal goals is not only vital to your growth as a strong woman and individual, but also will help to make you an even better mother.

So if you find yourself stuck between a rock and a hard place right now, wondering if you can still become the person you dreamed about becoming before those two lines showed up, allow me to assure you.

You *can* still become her.

You'll just tack on the title of "Mom" while you get there.

CHAPTER THREE

What Do I Say?
How to Tell Your Parents

~~~~~~

The day after I took my pregnancy test, after calling two different doctors for a blood test because I was *sure* there was a mistake and being laughed off twice, I decided to visit my campus health center at Saginaw Valley State University in Michigan. Although I found some pretty credible sources online that assured me using a cup with soap in it could result in a false positive, both offices refused to see me. Apparently, if your period is late and you have administered two or more positive home pregnancy tests, there is a pretty good chance you are pregnant. Who knew?

It took me a good thirty minutes of pacing up and down the hall next to the health center door, walking in and out twice, and reading every brochure outside before I finally worked up the courage to go inside and ask for a test. After taking yet another test, the nurse-practitioner called me into her office for the results, and there was no denying it any longer. I was definitely pregnant. When she began asking me how I would tell my parents—the one thing I feared the most—I broke down in tears. I sat in the chair, sobbing uncontrollably, while she examined her chart in silence. After about a minute or two of discomfort on her part and utter devastation on mine, she stood up and announced:

"I have other patients to see, but you can stay here if you want."

And so this woman, after delivering the verdict that changed my life forever, walked out on me without so much as a backward glance—or even a Kleenex. I later learned that she justified her hasty departure by claiming that she had a "more urgent" case than mine—a young man with a sore throat.

So I learned that I was on my own and, even more frightening, never to be alone again. I knew I needed help to face the pregnancy, which for me meant telling my parents, a moment that caused me more anxiety than giving birth. How do you look your dad in the eyes and tell him what you have (gasp) done?

You don't. Or rather, you don't if you are me. I courageously told my parents over the phone!

> You'll know best how to break the news to your parents, but however you choose, my one piece of advice is to do it sooner rather than later.

It may sound cowardly, and perhaps it was, but I did have my reasons for doing it that way. My family practices the Catholic faith, and I wanted to give my parents time to react before seeing me in person. Logistically, Ben and I were up at college at the time and wouldn't be home for another weekend, so it made sense to allow the news to settle before we met them face-to-face.

Plus, as I said, I was scared.

Many of my friends chose to tell their parents directly, and it worked out fine for them. You'll know best how to break the news to your parents, but however you choose, my one piece of advice is to do it sooner rather than later. I can tell you that the stress and dread I experienced about telling them was much worse than actually telling them. Furthermore, their reactions may surprise you, as was the case with me.

"I'm just going to do it," I said to Ben one morning while perched in his truck as we ran some errands. I grabbed my cell phone and held it up for emphasis. "Right now. I'm just going to call them and get it over with."

"No!" Ben cried. "Do not tell them, not yet, not over the phone."

"Why?" I asked calmly. "We are going home this weekend anyway. I'll tell them now, and they'll have time to process the news before they see us in person. It will be better this way."

I don't think I convinced either one of us with this reasoning; nevertheless, I let my stomach return from my throat to its proper place and hit my mom's speed dial, number two. I felt the phone begin to heat my ear as I struggled to breathe normally.

"Hell-*o*," my mom answered in her sing-song voice.

"Mum, put Dad on the phone with you."

Muffled sounds and mumbles ensued as my dad picked up the basement phone.

When I had them both on the line, I took a deep breath.

"Okay, there is no easy way to say this, so I'm just going to do it," I said, the words bursting out of me as much as my rapidly expanding belly.

"I'm pregnant."

Silence.

And then. Laughter.

Upon hearing that she was to be a grandmother, that her twenty-one-year-old daughter had become pregnant out of wedlock, my mother actually laughed. Granted, I think it was mostly nervous and shocked laughter, but still, laughter was not exactly the reaction I had expected.

"Do you think you are the first person this has happened to?" my mom asked, in between giggles. "I'm practically the only one in my family who *wasn't* pregnant before the wedding!"

My mom's matter-of-fact reaction was just what I needed to hear. Her joking revelation of unplanned pregnancy as a genetic issue in my family soon turned my tears into shaky laughter. She helped me to see the pregnancy for what it was—not a terrible thing. I wasn't calling her to tell her I was sick or to deliver some other dreadful news. She put things into perspective by reminding me that I was certainly not the first person this had happened to, nor would I be the last. And most importantly, she didn't judge me, nor did she offer me any advice. She knew this was my decision and that to accept it, I would need to find my own strength.

But it still isn't exactly an easy thing to break to your parents.

> I would need to find
> my own strength.

Lianne Cole, now the mother of three, found out she was pregnant at age twenty-one, and she and her boyfriend struggled to tell her parents. "There we were, two scared kids, still in college, without any real jobs, about to have a baby," she said. "The thought terrified us, and honestly, we felt it was a hopeless situation." Lianne's parents were very religious, and she dreaded telling them. "The last thing I wanted to do was to bring shame on them," confessed Lianne. For months, she hid her pregnancy from everyone, until one day when her mom found her prenatal vitamins. "Turns out trying to hide prenatal vitamins in my suitcase was not such a smart idea," Lianne said jokingly.

Raquel Kato, a young mom who has an incredibly similar story to mine (we're both Catholic, became pregnant at twenty-one, *and* our daughters have almost the same name!) shares her story of telling her parents:

I remember crying and crying and crying and repeatedly trying to convince myself I had enough strength to tell my parents. I finally had one tiny moment of courage, and I knew it wouldn't last long, so I decided to call my mom first. I remember feeling like the phone rang for an eternity. No answer. I called again. No answer. I was freaking out! How could she not answer? Then, a few minutes later my phone started to ring. It was my mom. I stared at the phone, about to ignore her call, scared, and about to cry. I answered. She knew right away something was wrong. I told her I had to tell her something, and if she was around people that she should go to another room. Then the floodgates opened. I bawled my eyes out and told her everything. Silence. Then— thank the Lord for my amazing mom—she said, "Oh, honey, I love you; it's going to be okay."

My worst fears were just wiped away. My mom did not abandon me, and she did not disown me. She did not hate me; instead she *loved* me. I was so blessed. Her response was just the first step in my healing process. After I got off the phone with my mom, my dad and brother walked into the house. I remember saying, "I'm so sorry I disappointed you." And my brother replied, "You haven't disappointed anyone because you made the right decision."

Mandy Lange was also fortunate enough to experience the unconditional support of her parents. "My parents had been noticing I was increasingly subdued each time I had visited (because of my guilty conscience)," says Mandy. "So my mom called me one day crying, asking why I was so depressed, and if it was her fault. I hated to do it over the phone, but I told her, and she responded, 'Is that it? You're just pregnant, not suicidal?' After we hung up, about a minute and a half later, my dad called to yell at me, asking why I wouldn't have told him sooner that he was a grandpa; he was actually excited! This was neither the reaction I expected nor the one I felt I deserved; I was still very upset with myself, but their support really helped me get through my guilt in the long run."

While some parents' reactions might be better than you could have ever hoped for, not all parents will have a positive reaction. My friend Meghan, whose daughter was born eight months after mine, experienced a not-so-positive reaction when she told her parents about her pregnancy. "My mom immediately started crying," Meghan remembers. "She cried for two straight weeks." And her dad's reaction? "My bedroom door still has a crack in it, from him hitting the door in frustration!" Meghan said.

> While some parents' reactions might be better than you could have ever hoped for, not all parents will have a positive reaction.

One mother, who asked to remain anonymous, was a young newlywed when she found herself unexpectedly expecting. "Here's the deal," she wrote. "When we decided to tell my parents I was pregnant, we wanted to sit them down and do it face to face. I called them up and invited them over, but my mother refused to come. She ended up refusing to speak to me throughout my pregnancy and even opted not to attend my baby shower, despite invitations sent to her. None of this was easy, but I think the hardest part was being pregnant and wondering: if I don't have a good mother, can I be a good mother? How will I know how to love this child as much as he or she needs to be loved when I wasn't loved enough?"

Jennifer Gomand Hiller was only fifteen when she became pregnant with her first child. After hiding the pregnancy for seven months, she finally told her mother about her baby, only to be devastated when her mother told her, "If that baby didn't have fingers and toes, we'd be at the [abortion] clinic."

Jennifer's father didn't take the news much better. "He told me I was a disgrace to his name," Jennifer told me in an e-mail. "It was hard. Thankfully, I had my best friend [for support]. Eventually my parents came around. It took my dad a little longer than my mom, but my relationship with him has never been the same. But I want young moms in my situation to know it's not the end of their world."

Melanie, a former high school classmate of mine, found out that she was expecting a baby with her boyfriend when she was twenty years old. "I was actually supposed to move back with my parents to Delaware," Melanie wrote me. "So it was very hard to tell them. After my first doctor's appointment, I told them. My dad told me he never wanted to talk to me again and my mom just cried and really didn't say anything to me for the next few days. It was hard being shunned."

Melanie's youngest two children have never even met their grandfather. "I feel like I did it on my own," Melanie said.

Feeling alone might very well be an anthem for young motherhood. "I had to learn early on that I had to become my best advocate," explains Gloria Malone, who became pregnant at the age of seventeen. "My mother was very much in shock and denial. So much so that she did not take me to see a doctor or start prenatal care until I was about three months along. I think for a long time she was angry, ashamed, felt guilty, and let down by my pregnancy but instead of openly expressing this, she would lash out in anger."

My other friend Megan (I know, I know, that's a lot to keep track of) who experienced an unplanned pregnancy right alongside me, didn't tell her parents about her pregnancy right away. "I was more scared about my parents' reaction than I was about having a baby," Megan remembers. So she waited. Until, one night, her parents left her a voice mail message while she was at dinner. They had heard "rumors." They wanted the truth. Megan laments not telling them sooner. "It was stupid not to," Megan says now, "But at the time, our relationship didn't make it easy."

Megan is adamant that telling your parents as soon as possible is the best idea. "If I could do it all over again, I would tell them right away. They deserve to know and hear it from you first."

Regardless of how the conversation with your parents may go, know this: The beauty in becoming a parent yourself is being able to take a step away from your own parents. It is amazing to find support, but you need to learn to take the bad with the good. Part of growing up as a parent is realizing that not everyone will agree with you all the time. You have to be your own person. Even more importantly, your life is not just your life anymore. It's not about just you, and that should impact your decision making more than your feelings. "Just do what you have to do," Melanie advises. "Unsupportive parents can be depressing, but [your] child is depending on you and only you. At that point it doesn't matter who approves. You have a human being to love and care for and you can only hope [your child] will grow to understand the sacrifices you have made."

> The beauty in becoming a parent yourself is being able to take a step away from your own parents.

There's that pesky word—*sacrifices*. There seems to be a lot of that when it comes to pregnancy and parenting. And in some cases, your sacrifice may come in the form of choosing adoption for your child because you lack the emotional and practical resources to raise your child yourself. Adoption is always an option, and it's a great one for the couples who are able to receive the child they always wanted. I'll never forget the bravery of one of my former patients who chose adoption for her baby. I held her hand as she wiped away tears, wondering if people would judge her for "giving her baby away." Watching her heart break as she did what she thought was best for her baby, I saw firsthand the beauty and courage in the sacrifice of a birthmother's heart.

No matter what you wind up doing or how you end up telling your parents, I hope you can find the strength you need to embrace your pregnancy, sacrifices and all, and find some source of support as you journey (or waddle) on.

Just remember this: you are never truly alone. There have been many young moms before you to deal with this, and there will be many after you, so stay strong. For all of us.

CHAPTER FOUR

What about Daddy? Things to Consider before You Tie the Knot

〜〜〜〜〜〜〜〜〜〜〜〜〜〜〜

Taking a break from our scenic bike ride, Ben and I stood on the rocky beach of the island, gazing through the drizzling rain at the water.

Turning to face me, Ben gingerly lowered himself down to one knee amongst the stones and pulled out a ring, the princess-cut diamond solitaire I had always dreamed of.

"Will you share the rest of your life with me? Will you become my wife?" he asked.

As the words left his mouth, the sun suddenly burst through the rain clouds, illuminating the profile of the man kneeling before me. Inadvertently, I brought my hand to my mouth, somehow still shocked by the moment, even though Ben's panicked pocket checks during our bike ride had clued me in to what was coming. A single tear slid down my cheek as I watched my new husband-to-be slide the delicate gold ring on my finger. We were completely isolated on a huge, rocky beach, surrounded by trees. At that moment, it felt like we were the only two people in the world as we kissed, and I admired my new diamond, glittering in the sunshine that seemed to embrace us.

The moment I became engaged was picture perfect. Except for one small detail:

I was two months pregnant.

While the biggest decisions most brides may make are where to host the wedding or how many people to invite, a much bigger decision loomed over me.

Which comes first? The baby carriage or marriage?

If you are in a relationship during your pregnancy, you will soon discover that friends, family, and even complete strangers will simply be dying to ask you one question: "So, are you guys going to get married now?"

As my friend Meaghan, a mother of two who is in a long-term relationship but not married, quipped, "That's just how it is. They look at you, they look at your child, and they look at your finger. We get it all the time."

Although it seems like there is a never-ending flow of celebrities getting married while they are pregnant, out here in the real world, a shotgun wedding still carries with it some degree of stigma, especially if, like me, you're from a relatively small town.

Any bride can tell you that planning a wedding is stressful. Throw a baby into the mix—before, during, or after the wedding—and the needle on the stress meter tends to rise quite a bit.

In marriage, there will be definitely be days when you think, "Why on earth did I ever get married?" You will want to stuff your husband's dirty socks down his throat and purposely hide his keys just to watch him panic, so the last thing you want is to doubt your entire marriage because of the baby.

Before you do anything else, take a moment to pause and really consider your circumstances. You don't want to make any rash decisions because of your pregnancy. Pregnancy alone is not a reason to rush into marriage, but it does necessitate a serious conversation about you and your boyfriend's future plans. Try taking some time apart from your boyfriend, with each of you coming to a decision before you discuss it together. Make sure you flip to the back of this book to review "*Early Mama's* Questions to Consider before Marriage" for some guidance.

> Pregnancy alone is not a reason to rush into marriage, but it does necessitate a serious conversation about you and your boyfriend's future plans.

Then, seek the counsel of someone you respect; if you are religious, I would suggest a pastor or priest, one that specializes in premarriage counseling. If you are Catholic, be sure to also look inside your heart and go to Confession—you will want a clean slate with God before you enter willingly into marriage. Trust me on that one. More on that later.

So, let's take a look at our options here, shall we?

Marriage before Carriage

For Ben and I, the marriage question wasn't really a question—we had already been planning marriage after college, and finding out I was pregnant put us in fast-forward mode. In my big Catholic family, the assumption was, of course, that we would get married as soon as possible. My mother, however, encouraged me to take my time and not rush into marriage because of the pregnancy. While she didn't want us living together, she also wanted to make sure I didn't enter into marriage before I was ready. She feared—as many God-fearing Catholic ladies do—that I would want to rush into marriage just to make things "right" again. But that's not what God wants. Marriage is a calling and a vocation, and entering into marriage for the wrong reasons, however well-intentioned, is a rocky foundation for any marriage.

I followed all my own advice here, and Ben and I ultimately came to the conclusion that it was important to us to become

> Marriage is a calling and a vocation, and entering into marriage for the wrong reasons, however well intentioned, is a rocky foundation for any marriage.

husband and wife before we took on the role of parents. And while I do feel it was the best decision, I won't lie to you when I say it was still hard for me to let go of my expectations of what my wedding was "supposed" to be like.

On one hand, I did want to get married. I wanted to be a wife before I became a mother. I wanted to not worry about being judged at the hospital, or having people looking at my ring finger, or having to write a different last name on my baby's birth certificate. But on the other hand, I can admit to you that I really just wanted my wedding to be about me. I wanted to feel pretty, not pukey. I wanted to have a bachelorette party. I wanted to drink and dance and make love on my wedding night. (In case you're wondering, I didn't have a bachelorette party. I didn't drink, I did dance, and no, I didn't make love on my wedding night; I fell asleep.)

All of those desires aside, I knew Ben was the man I wanted to marry. I just didn't know how to let go of my picture-perfect expectations for my wedding. And this is where the fact that I am lucky enough to have the chance to write a book comes in handy—because I can tell you that if you are feeling the same way, it's okay. It's normal and natural for you to want your picture-perfect wedding. I mean, the idea of happily ever after is only drilled into us from the age of two, right? So don't let anyone tell you to suck it up because it's your fault for having sex or that you are being selfish, because it's not, and you're not.

A little—okay, a *big*—part of me, felt like I didn't deserve my dream wedding because I had sinned and had premarital sex. I felt like I couldn't really tell anyone how I was feeling, because well, they all thought I had sinned by having premarital sex. But since you are no different from me, I can say: you do deserve to have the wedding of your dreams.

I just don't want you to let anyone else define what a "dream" wedding is supposed to look like.

If you know, deep down, that choosing marriage before your baby is born is the right choice for you, then go for it. Let yourself feel sad about letting go of the expectations of what you always imagined your wedding would be, but don't let the mourning overshadow your wedding. Don't let anyone make you feel less beautiful, less worthy, or less like a bride. Because you *are* beautiful, and you *are* worthy, and you will be the most perfect bride to ever walk down that aisle. I can guarantee you that any guilt you are feeling is completely unfounded—God *wants* you to have a nice wedding and he may even (gasp) want you to wear that white dress, no matter what any grumpy great-aunt says about you. If you've made things right with God, wear that white dress proudly and without shame, because your soul is as pure as that beating heart in your belly. And that's all that matters.

> If you've made things right with God, wear that white dress proudly and without shame, because your soul is as pure as that beating heart in your belly. And that's all that matters.

A wedding as a pregnant bride carries its own form of beauty; already, you are one with your spouse, and you are living the proclamation of your love for each other as you literally grow your family.

If you have received the sacrament of Reconciliation and have completed your premarital classes with your priest, then you have nothing to be ashamed of. And in a way, a family wedding means accepting the ultimate lesson of your unplanned pregnancy—that even when things don't necessarily go the way you planned, they may just become the most incredible experiences of your lives.

I think we sometimes place too much importance on being a bride and having the perfect wedding when that's not what a marriage is about. As my cousin and fellow pregnant bride Mandy says, "Don't forget that your marriage is about your commitment to your husband, not your baby—so don't let people tell you otherwise."

I became a pregnant bride four days after Christmas. At five months pregnant, after two months of planning, I walked down the aisle. Four hundred guests craned their necks to look at me, not just to see the blushing bride or beautiful dress, but also to see if I was starting to *show.* I blubbered my way through our vows and was shocked when our hour-and-a-half long wedding Mass flew by. I sipped a teensy bit of champagne in our limo ride and faked it with sparkling grape juice at the reception. I didn't worry about what the guests at our reception thought about my baby bump. I danced the night away, swollen feet and all. I practically swam in the delicious double-chocolate fountains someone gifted us with at our dessert table. I kissed my new husband, and I can honestly say after all of my misgivings, and even with the occasional pang of regret I will feel in attending other "normal" weddings, that my wedding day was beautiful.

While beautiful, planning a wedding at high speed while fighting morning sickness and losing the ability to button my pants was also an incredibly stressful time. So, if you decide to join me in taking the marriage before carriage plunge, here are a few tips I am passing along that I learned from my graceful, pregnant walk down the aisle:

- **Remember that there is no "right" or "wrong" way to have a wedding.** The wedding police will not come and shut you down if you choose to do things differently. I didn't have the time or energy (okay, or money!) for favors or programs, so I skipped them. Do you think anyone remembers? Focus on what is important to *you*. I felt like a lot of people wanted us to have a traditional wedding, but the fact it is, I was not a traditional bride. Although I didn't know it at the time, that was okay! You don't have to pretend to be something that you are not. You can be a beautiful pregnant bride and still have an amazing wedding. My cousin Mandy actually made her pregnancy a part of her wedding; she chose a blue garter to wear under her dress to reveal her baby's gender to her new husband and wedding guests—*adorable*.

- **Don't let anyone make you feel that you don't deserve everything a "normal" bride gets.** The white dress, the showers, the parties—you deserve it all! Talk to your girl-friends, and talk to your family, and let them know what's important to you. You may not care about having a bach-elorette party, but maybe the bridal shower is something you've dreamed about. Don't be afraid to ask for the events that will make you feel like a bride.

- **Accept help.** This one's a biggie. I had so much help with my wedding, and it was wonderful. Normally, I am a person who loves to plan. Really. I am one of those crazy people who plans things for fun and writes to-do lists with things I have already done just so I can cross them off, but when it came to my wedding, I learned to just say "thank you." Whether they felt sorry for me or just really loved me, I found that a lot of people wanted to help us pull off our wedding. So,

I learned to accept help. Plus, if you do the pregnant bride thing, there will come a time when you will need help with that dress. Remember, pregnant women pee a lot.

- **Find a seamstress.** And if you can't find one, e-mail me, and I will help you contact mine. A seamstress to a pregnant bride is what coffee is to the morning—absolutely necessary. I bought my wedding dress five sizes too large and had multiple fittings and adjustments. On the eve of my wedding, I found myself doing one last, final fitting, my sisters and mother crowded around me. My mom zipped the dress behind me . . . and I heard a thunderous *rriiippppp*. My dress, let out twice already, tore completely down the side with hours to go before the ceremony. And that's when I turned, sobbing and hysterical, to an angel-turned-seamstress named Mary Jane, who worked an overnight miracle to allow me to walk down the aisle and become a married woman.

- **Wear comfy shoes.** Pregnant ankles and dainty bridal shoes do not a merry match make. With all the dancing and long hours on your feet on your wedding day, you want to be sure that you are comfortable. Try on your shoes at the end of the day, too, when your feet are a swollen mess. I recommend online shopping for cute and comfy flats. I actually recommend online shopping for everything when you are pregnant. It's easier. And I recommend online shopping after the baby comes, too. Let's just thank God for the Internet, and call it a day.

I can say that I never thought my wedding would turn out the way it did. I never thought that I would show up to the start of my marriage with a baby under my magic gown. But then again, sometimes you have to rewrite the fairy tale.

Carriage before Marriage

My friend Megan (the Cedar Point one, remember?) also debated the marriage question. But unlike our hometown priest, who may have pulled a few strings to allow us to say "I do" with only two months of planning, Megan's parish refused to marry her without the requisite six-month waiting period. "We called a couple of churches," Megan said, "But we were flat out told that they didn't marry people who have kids before they are married. The other said they wouldn't because we were pregnant. It was almost a relief to be told no."

I had the honor of being Megan's bridesmaid as she walked down the aisle in the fall after her son was born. She had a beautiful fall wedding, and her son was purposely not a part of the ceremony. "I wanted it to be about us," Megan explained. "It was perfect. I wouldn't have had it any other way."

My cousin-in-law Jacquelyn also decided against the pregnant walk down the aisle, opting instead to wed after her son, Eli, was born. "It's hard to narrow it down to one primary reason why I decided to wait until after I had Eli to get married," Jacquelyn said. "But it was mainly because I wanted to be sure I was entering into marriage for the right reasons. Finding out about Eli was definitely a blessing, but it was also a surprise. I didn't want to rush into a wedding while I was trying to figure out a life that was best for my baby, my (now) husband, and myself. With the situation we were in, we knew we loved each other; but we wanted to be sure that our relationship was ready for marriage, especially after a baby came along."

Kelly Smith was barely eighteen when her daughter was born, so she decided to wait to get married. "Neither of us felt the need to rush a wedding simply because we had a baby," says Kelly. "We both knew we weren't ready to be husband and wife and decided to focus solely on our daughter rather than trying to figure out a marriage, too." When their daughter was five, Kelly and her husband finally said "I do" in a very simple, casual ceremony at the courthouse. They will celebrate twelve years this year and Kelly says they are "as happy as ever."

Hollie Thompson waited until her daughter was six months old to have the wedding, but called it a hard decision. "[My daughter] cut her first two teeth the night before the wedding," Hollie said. "She spent most of the day crying her eyes out, and my sister had to miss my wedding to try to calm down my daughter in another room." Hollie recommends considering either getting married before the baby comes or waiting until the baby is walking. "It will make things a little easier," she says.

Heather Craven had a difficult experience feeling pressured into marriage—which ultimately resulted in a divorce after ten years. She was seven-and-a-half months pregnant when she and her boyfriend got married in a small ceremony. "We both wanted to wait," says Heather. "But there was so much pressure from his dad. I always felt like our marriage wasn't ours."

Heather and her husband would have celebrated twenty-one years this year. "If we were to go back I believe we would have waited until we were both ready for marriage," Heather confesses. "Pregnancy is such a time of upheaval, and for us adding marriage was too much."

Considerations

For the bride who is contemplating the pregnant versus the postpartum walk down the aisle, here are some considerations:

- **Breast-feeding**. The thought of disrobing out of your wedding gown to nurse an infant in the middle of the chicken dance at your reception may be a deal breaker. For some women, like Jacquelyn, who nursed her baby in a closet while her mom held her dress, it's no big deal. Consider the age your baby will be at your wedding. A newborn requires feedings every two to three hours, while after the age of four months, frequency of breast-feeding reduces to about four or five feedings a day. Pumping, while not romantic, would also get the job done. Scout out the ceremony and reception sites for a private place with proper electrical outlets for your breast pump. And as Jacquelyn pointed out, it was slightly unromantic to "whip out the breast pump" as soon as she and her new husband arrived at their wedding-night hotel; but, she said, "I know my husband loves me and thinks I'm beautiful—the unromantic parts are part of marriage, too."

- **Child Care**. You should think about the care of your child during your wedding and ceremony. Do you have a family member who can care for the baby through it all? Is there a quiet place for the baby to nap? Jacquelyn accomplished this feat quite nicely, with family members trading on and off throughout the day. She even incorporated her son into the ceremony, with the groom holding their six-month-old as she walked down the aisle toward both of her men. Unfortunately, her son was cutting his first tooth that day and cried the entire time, but it was still adorable. "While Eli was definitely on my mind all night," Jacquelyn said, "I knew he was in good hands, and I was able to have a good time at my wedding."

- **Your Body**. Sorry ladies, but we have to talk about it. Fortunately, you should know that all women gain weight differently during pregnancy. Unfortunately, if this is your first pregnancy, you may gain more weight than with subsequent pregnancies. With weight gain often comes swelling, so also consider the wedding ring. Toward the end of my first pregnancy, I had to replace my wedding ring with a larger substitute ring because my fingers were so swollen. A ring resize may be necessary after you deliver, or a "dummy" ring could be used in the ceremony. And then, there's finding the dress: the magical moment when your closest girlfriends gather around you in awe as you twirl gracefully in front of the gently lit mirror that highlights your beauty. Or, if you're me, you wind up puking in the parking lot of the dress store and buying the first dress you try on. Either way, you'll have a dress!

- **Outside Pressures**. You probably know by now that many people will have opinions on how you ought to parent. From breast-feeding to pacifiers to diapers, you can count on everyone putting in their own two cents. The topic of marriage will be no different. I heard it all: My mom urged me to not to rush into marriage, while plenty of others said things like, "Of course you'll get married right now, you can't keep living in sin!" With so many opinions and pressure from people you love and genuinely want to please (such as your parents), you may need to take time to get away and focus on what *you* want.

  Meagan Francis and her boyfriend got married when she became pregnant at nineteen. "I got so much pressure from all sides. My dad insisted I marry Jon. My mom insisted I not marry Jon. (She even got her pastor to call me to try to talk me out of it.) His parents were just really disappointed. It was a really stressful time for me."

Unfortunately, Meagan and her husband ended up in divorce court. "We did what we thought other people wanted us to do, which didn't make either of us happy, and we took it out on each other," she says. "The biggest factor in our divorce, though, was that neither of us took full responsibility for our lives right away." Happily, after working on some issues, Meagan and her husband eventually remarried and have a healthy and strong marriage today.

Jacquelyn experienced many of the pressures that I did—we share some of the same family, after all—but while I lived very near to family, she lived out of state. "[Getting away] was huge," said Jacquelyn. "I needed the mind-set that this was my wedding day and to not worry about what other people thought."

- **Resources**. Consider the emotional, financial, and physical resources needed to plan a wedding. Depending on the size of your dream wedding, it may be an involved and lengthy process, and you will need to decide how you can handle the planning and work involved. With school, work, and my pregnancy, I found that I just couldn't summon the energy to plan all the details of the wedding we had. We invited hundreds of guests. My solution? I learned to say "thank you." Family and friends stepped forward to help with previously undiscovered talents; an uncle took the photos, an aunt made my wedding cake, and the lady I used to babysit for arranged flowers. We ended up with so many gifts of time and talent at our wedding, and it made the night meaningful for everyone.

On the other hand, it was important for Jacquelyn to be involved in planning her wedding. Waiting until after Eli, she said that she "had time to plan things out, and I got to do things how I wanted. I purposefully chose that." She had the wedding that she wanted and was able to be a part of it every step of the way.

- **Your New Normal.** This one is important, so pay attention. Before you decide to get married, and especially if you decide to get married as a pregnant bride, you need to understand that there is no such thing as "normal." As a twenty-one-year-old, pregnant bride, I felt like no one really knew what to do with me; I didn't have a bachelorette party or a bridal shower. I didn't question the lack of "normal' bridal activities, because I didn't think I deserved them. I was wrong. Please learn from my experience and realize that as a pregnant bride or as a mother, you *do* deserve it all.

  Jacquelyn didn't have a bridal shower (her choice), but she did have a bachelorette party. "I needed that time with my girls. I even brought Eli along for the weekend and hired my brother to watch him when we went out. I knew this was the only time I would do this, so I tried to make the best out of the situation."

A Word about the Honeymoon

While it's not a necessity, of course, taking a honeymoon is an important part of the wedding to many couples. Ben and I were gifted with a trip to a family timeshare, so we did take advantage of a post-wedding honeymoon. It was really nice to have that time as a couple before the baby arrived, but I definitely struggled with enjoying it. Parasailing, horseback riding on the beach, and even drinks with my new husband were all out of the question during our tropical getaway. Instead of locking ourselves in our room for some newlywed time, I was falling asleep at the pool and enjoying little old ladies commenting on my baby bump for the first time.

While I lounged about with a virgin strawberry daiquiri in hand, my pregnant body stuffed into a bikini and stretched out on the sand, I definitely looked more like Shamu than a sexy new wife. I will say that I'm glad we got away, but my honeymoon was hard for me to enjoy. I felt so guilty for feeling too exhausted to move and once again, for ruining what was supposed to be the best sex of our lives by taking a free sample early. It was not the honeymoon I envisioned, for sure, but we've already started saving for our next honeymoon someday, when we can rekindle the romance. Although, sadly, my bikini will not be making a reappearance.

While I tried to enjoy a last pre-baby vacation, Jacquelyn took a "familymoon," tagging along on her husband's scheduled work trip to Disney World. And last fall, Jacquelyn and her husband took a "real" honeymoon—a once-in-a-lifetime trip to Italy for twelve days.

Some couples keep it simple, like Mandy, who opted to enjoy an overnight stay at a hotel near her hometown. She and her new husband, along with her baby bump, enjoyed a quiet night relaxing and a baseball game the next day. "We chose a honeymoon close to home because it was cheaper than going somewhere," said Mandy. "I don't think I would have had fun if we went to a resort because I was still feeling nauseated all the time. I don't regret staying around; we had a great time relaxing and doing fun things we wouldn't normally justify doing, like getting good seats to a baseball game or going out to a really nice restaurant."

Even for couples who aren't pregnant (who are these people any-way?), it's becoming popular to delay the honeymoon until a year or so into the marriage. Just be sure you diligently set aside money and actually go, or life has a way of catching you off guard! As with the wedding, keep in mind that there is no one "right" way to do things, so pick what is important to you regarding a honeymoon and just go with it. Anne Dziekońska and her husband Marek, who it should be noted, did not have a baby until well into their marriage, still chose to delay their honeymoon until four years into their mar-riage. Anne says, "As it's not always an option for newlyweds to go on their honeymoon right away, my advice to them would be: never, ever feel guilty about taking that honeymoon! Save up money, have fun planning and most importantly, actually take your honeymoon! A honeymoon is more than money spent on fun, it's an investment in your lifelong commitment to your spouse, to your marriage, and your family."

In the end, whether you choose to get married before you have your baby, wait until the baby is born, or if you are not in a com-mitted relationship, I encourage you to seek some spiritual counsel and consider what is best for both you and your child.

If we can take a serious detour here, it's important to discuss that even parents who are not in a committed relationship still need to work together to forge a life together. Lauren Furneaux's story illus-trates the importance of this more than anything. Lauren is a young mom whose daughter Lily was born only three days apart from Ada—I can still remember the joy in Lily's eyes when they played together. Tragically, Lauren struggled for custody with Lily's father throughout her entire life, until Lily was murdered at the hands of her stepmother in the fall of 2010. Lily was only two years old.

"I couldn't do anything about Lily being in the care of people I not only didn't like but didn't trust," Lauren explained. "So in co-parenting situations, parents need to understand the importance of getting along. Communicate, because for the next eighteen years, and for the rest of your life, the other biological parent has rights to that child."

Today, Lauren has started a nonprofit organization called Justice for Lily to bring awareness of the issue of child abuse and to advise other parents on the legal aspects of advocating for their children. "We want to help point people in the right direction, since no one was there to do that for us," said Lauren.

Lily, the heartbreaking sight of her tiny pink coffin, and the sounds of Lauren's sobs trailing behind her are forever emblazoned in my mind. Lauren has endured what no mother should ever have to, and she is, quite simply, one of the strongest women I know. "I don't know what I would do without my Catholic faith," Lauren said. "After losing a child, you have a closeness to God that you can't explain. I am no longer afraid of what is to come, and I live my life in a way to make both God and Lily proud. I know that she is waiting for me on the other side. That day will be an amazing day, but until then I will fight until my dying breath to save other children."

And although Lily's story is so difficult to hear, I include it to illustrate the importance of placing our focus, as mothers, on what really does matter. It's not the perfect wedding dress or the Pinterest-worthy floral centerpieces.

It's about love and faith and holding on to your future—*as a family.*

CHAPTER FIVE

What Did I Do? Navigating Your Feelings of Guilt

With the sudden appearance of those two blue lines on my pregnancy test, I was introduced to the old standby of unmarried, pregnant women everywhere—guilt. I felt tremendous guilt about *everything*. Guilt for having sex, guilt for getting caught, guilt for getting pregnant, guilt for not living up to my standards as a daughter and sister, guilt for being sad that I was pregnant, guilt for my boyfriend's sake, and even, ridiculously, guilt for feeling guilty.

Yes, it got a little out of hand. But the fact is that all that guilt made it almost impossible for me to get through my pregnancy.

Perhaps you are nothing like me and have escaped feeling any guilt about your pregnancy. But if, by some chance, you are like me and have the tiniest smidge of guilt, then, please, by all means, read on.

The truth is, I'm religious. I grew up with nine years of Catholic school, I said my prayers out of a little booklet during my early college years, and I have genuinely sought a relationship with God. My faith has always been important to me. Not only did I believe that sex should be reserved for marriage for personal reasons, but my lifelong Catholic faith also maintained that belief. It may sound old-fashioned now, but Ben and I really did want to wait until we were married to have sex. It felt like we fought against it—and then failed.

This is how I came to view my whole start to motherhood.

As a failure.

I truly felt like having premarital sex was the ultimate deal breaker. Premarital sex was the sin that I would never recover from. Its repercussions would touch everything in my life. My baby would be forever marked by my sin. Surely she would be emotionally messed up, or our lives would never be quite right, scarred by a marriage that started out badly. Surely I would never love her the way a "real" planned mother would.

I was petrified that in creating this little person before marriage, essentially thwarting God's plans for her and bringing her into the world before her time, I had somehow ruined her life. We shouldn't have had sex; therefore, she shouldn't be here yet . . . right?

My guilt culminated when one night, right before Christmas, I found myself at church standing next to an older, married, successful woman who had been told that she could never bear children. After more than ten years of infertility and an adoption, she had just discovered that she was pregnant. There we stood, two women with unplanned pregnancies. Both beginning to show, we were just weeks apart. Person after person walked up to her and congratulated her on her "miracle from God." As they moved on past her, a few people met my eyes but quickly looked down. Not one person congratulated me.

It was hard to overcome the thought that my baby should have never happened. I had always dreamed of becoming a mom. I had envisioned how I would tell my future husband about our upcoming bundle of joy. It was all planned out in my mind—a whole meal out of baby foods: baby carrots, baby potatoes, baby steaks. (For some reason, I was also convinced that this was an original idea.) I pictured my husband's puzzled face as I presented each dish, his shock and excitement when realization finally dawned. What I didn't picture was finding out I was a mother in the kitchen of my student apartment at 3 o'clock in the morning, crying hysterically while my boyfriend sat motionless in the corner. So much for those baby carrots.

On top of all my other guilt for having sex and getting pregnant, I even felt guilt for even considering the fact that I could celebrate my pregnancy. Who would be happy about a college student getting pregnant? The consensus around me seemed to be that this baby was, if not a downright mistake, at the very *least*, certainly bad timing.

The guilt about my sin was overwhelming and exhausting. The truth is that I was so all-consumed by my guilt that I avoided even thinking about my baby. I kept busy with school and classes so that I could keep my mind off the small person

> The truth is that I was so all-consumed by my guilt that I avoided even thinking about my baby.

growing inside me. And when she grew big enough that I could start to feel her, instead of delight and excitement at those first butterfly kicks, I felt a wave of panic—feeling her just made it all too real for my liking. I was too trapped in a sinkhole of darkness to even enjoy my own baby.

A Prayerful Revelation

As all of this was going on, I was knee-deep in my wedding preparations. I knew that I needed help to accept my baby and get over my guilt before I could freely and happily become a married woman. And so, out of desperation, I started to pray. Every day, for months and months and months, I prayed. My wedding loomed closer and closer while my belly grew larger and larger.

I felt nothing at first. I still felt wracked with guilt, self-doubt, and despair. Sometimes I prayed the Rosary before bed. I would usually fall asleep near the end, but it's the thought that counts, right? St. Thérèse of Lisieux, the Little Flower, once said that God loves to see us fall asleep during prayers—just like we love watching our kids fall asleep. So I just go with that. Sometimes, my prayers would lack words or structure, but they found their way into the universe as desperate pleas for help. No matter their form, my prayers felt like they were radiating from my core; my entire soul was in constant pleading with God. I wanted to believe that I could love my baby. I wanted to believe that this baby could be a good thing or even—dare to dream—meant to be.

Finally, when our wedding loomed a mere four weeks away, it happened. For the first time in my life, I felt God speak to me—something I had only read about, but never actually experienced. And before you go thinking I'm all kinds of crazy, I will swear on my life that it's something that has never happened to me before and something I haven't experienced since. I'm not someone who goes around in constant communication with God.

I was plopped down on my favorite couch of the time, a lovely cream-colored contraption with swirled raspberry accents that my mother had handed down to me and that I frequented throughout my pregnancy. Dusk was just creeping in through the window and across the vintage sitting room of the old apartment that I rented. I sipped a cup of decaf tea and watched my fake fireplace log twirl around, glowing with the aid of an ancient light bulb and making a crackling, rustling sound with what appeared to be tinfoil wrapped around it.

I was thinking, as I normally did for about twenty-three hours a day, about my pregnancy, about what I had done, about how much my life had changed, about how this baby still didn't feel real to me. And suddenly, right there, in a one-hundred-year-old living room on a hand-me-down couch, I was given a very clear, very real answer: *My baby was not a punishment.*

I heard it as clearly as if God himself had swooped down in front of that fake swirling fireplace with me. It was a voice that at once seemed to fill the room and come from within me. I felt his words like an imprint on my heart—a realization that was so simple, and yet changed everything for me in an instant.

I realized immediately that I could not grasp the concept that even after what I had done—having premarital sex, mocking God with an act that was ugly and selfish—he could still bless me with something as profound as a baby.

I realized I was waiting for my punishment. I wanted to be punished for what I had done. I felt so guilty about having sex that I was cowering in fear, like the old story of Adam and Eve, hiding my

> I felt so guilty about having sex that I was cowering in fear.

nakedness in shame, wallowing in self-pity and not trusting God in any way, shape, or form. I felt like I couldn't possibly deserve any happiness from this child. I didn't believe I could love my baby, because I didn't believe God loved me anymore.

And then God took my understanding one step further. List-checker that I am, he took the time to spell it out for me, helping me to see exactly how this baby came to be:

My baby was sent to teach me true love.

I felt God reveal to me that—lo and behold—he really didn't hate me for what I had done. He understood that my boyfriend and I had truly loved each other, but that we had been misguided in our expression of love. We thought that sex meant that we "really" loved each other. He saw that we needed a little help in understanding what true love is all about. So he gave us the opportunity to learn the truest and most selfless form of love—parenthood. Because, after all, what else provides a faster lesson in true and selfless love than a baby?

[Forehead smack.]

When I finally understood God's plan for me and my baby, it was the biggest sense of peace that I have ever felt. Relief and joy filled my heart as the fake fireplace became a blurred vision of tinfoil and bad lighting through my tears. I finally realized how my baby could be a "good" thing coming out of a "bad" thing. I felt as if I had permission to love my baby, and that it was okay to be happy about my unplanned pregnancy. And that, my friends, was the game changer.

God didn't punish me with a baby. Yes, I had sinned, but he still loved me. He wasn't about to give up on me so easily. I could start over, begin a new life, and it could still be all I had dreamed about. I could still be that cool mom with the craft cupboard I had once planned on, still love my cute husband, and still feel proud of where I had come in my life.

I was no longer hiding behind my sin, cringing and waiting for the blow I felt was sure to come. I felt like I could finally hold my head high in the knowledge that God loved me, God loved my baby, and that he was with me on this new path. It was such an incredible gift to feel the guilt lifted off of me.

I was able—finally able—to make my way back to God through confession and through our premarital classes. With a clean soul and a loving heart, I could walk down the aisle to become a married woman before we welcomed our daughter into the world.

The Original Young Mother

Now, let's rewind to that night at the church. Remember when I was standing next to the lady with the "miracle" pregnancy? Well, that night happened to be a Christmas Mass. The church was warm and cozy, decorated with boughs of holly, and good tidings of cheer were spread all around. Meanwhile, I was feeling fat and miserable in the pew of my soon-to-be husband's small-town church. I felt like everyone was looking at me. *"Oh, there's Chaunie, the good girl that got pregnant [snicker, snicker]."* I sat, generally feeling sorry for myself and willing my belly to look flat, while the priest started his sermon.

That night, the priest highlighted the fact that God works in mysterious ways—and that God is deliberate. He could have paved the way for Jesus to enter the world in any way, shape, or form. And yet he chose Mary—a poor, pregnant, unwed teenager.

Let's think about that for a second. I'll never know if the priest that night was talking directly to me or not, but his words felt like a second chance.

And while I'm pretty sure no one would buy my excuse that I, too, had experienced a miraculous conception (tried it), it hit me that it was possible, just possible, that I may have more in common with Mary than I realized.

> It hit me that it was possible, just possible, that I may have more in common with Mary than I realized.

Do you think she wasn't judged?

Do you think everyone really believed that she was carrying the Son of God?

Do you think she didn't have to struggle with self-doubt and insecurity?

Can't you just picture a scene from her life—all the old ladies of the village, clad in their robes, standing around the watering hole, clucking their tongues in disapproval at Mary as she made her way over with her clay jug?

"Oh, there's Mary. Did you hear she's pregnant? Claims it was by the Holy Spirit. Sure. Right. And I'm Pontius Pilate!" [laughs all around].

Mary was the original young mom. She trusted God with her unplanned pregnancy, even at the risk of persecution and death. (No, really, did you know that legally, Joseph could have stoned her to death for getting pregnant before they were married? Somehow, I never realized that, but in short, Mary is awesome.) Instead of despairing, Mary chose to draw strength from her faith and God's plan for her instead of focusing on the naysayers.

> Mary was the original young mom.

Sitting in the pew that night, I felt a connection with Mary. I knew that she had, in some small way, felt some of the fears, misgivings, and judgments that I was having about my unplanned pregnancy. It was such a comfort to me to think that maybe, just maybe, God had chosen Mary and placed her in a situation that looked pretty bad—an unmarried, pregnant, teenager—just to teach us all that things are not always what they seem. There are no accidents with God, and life is always an intentional gift.

Maybe it's wishful thinking on my part, but I like to think that God was making a point. Life, in the literal and figurative sense, doesn't always follow the plan we thought it would. But ultimately, God is always in control, and he really does have a plan. Who would have guessed that the Savior would be born to a fourteen-year-old unwed mother? While I am clearly under no assumptions that I am carrying divine children in my womb, although I happen to think they are pretty cool kids, I have to say that the realization that I was not alone in the whole unplanned pregnancy and young-mom thing was pretty comforting. Even the Mother of God had to go through it—very good company in this journey, when you think about it.

Raquel Kato explained how she used her devotion to Mary as a guide to becoming a mother after her pregnancy, too. "Being a mom means imitating the Virgin Mary," Raquel said. "Mary was strong, yet she expressed her strength with grace and compassion. She sacrificed her entire life for her son, and she never abandoned him. She taught him love and protected him, and then let him choose his destiny without hindering his growth. In the end, being a mom means doing everything in your power to show your children what true, genuine, authentic love is, so that they can learn to do the same."

No one knows what your personal relationship is with God. No one knows your story, what you have gone through, or what is to come. This is your journey, and no one can make it for you. If you are struggling

> This is your journey, and no one can make it for you.

with guilt and shame about your pregnancy, I will say that I get it—and I hope that you will find the strength to ask for help in whatever spiritual way works for you. My fellow Catholics, go to Confession, pray to Mary, and speak with a priest. I have a friend who is a single mom. She prays to St. Jude, patron saint of lost causes. "I ask him to help me out all the time!" she laughs.

You need to get that guilt and shame off of your chest—because before you know it, there will be a baby there instead. You may even find your heart changed forever. Raquel felt so much guilt and shame about her pregnancy that she actually scheduled an abortion. "I felt dirty, and unlovable, and ashamed beyond belief. I felt like such a hypocrite, and that if anyone knew, they would abandon me. So, I chose not to tell a single soul and scheduled an abortion. I chose to be selfish and protect my reputation and future. Thank God, literally, a week before that appointment, the Lord pierced my heart with his unconditional love, mercy, grace, and forgiveness. He did this at Mass, through the Eucharist, and gave me the courage to cancel my abortion, and tell my family and friends I was pregnant. Now I have a beautiful little girl to love forever."

The same guilt that threatened to drive Raquel to the abortion clinic can be suffocating for women facing unplanned pregnancies outside of marriage. It can keep you from your normal activities, especially if you participate in any religious or spiritual activities, such as attending church or even praying. Going to church or doing other spiritual acts forces you to face your own guilt and feelings as well as face others who may be judging you. It's not easy. One young-mommy blogger commented that she had the same feelings with her first pregnancy. "I quit going to church because I was so ashamed," she said. "It took a while before I learned to embrace it."

Finding a Way to Worship When You Feel Judged

It's hard, because even when you are trying to make your own peace with your pregnancy, the very act of going to public places of worship can feel like a setback when people look down on you for being young, unmarried, and pregnant. Having gone through it, my advice is simply to give yourself time, but *do not give up*. You have nothing to be ashamed of. Everyone is different, and it is important to continue to follow the spiritual practices that are meaningful to you, even if it's hard at first. I would also encourage you to look into different outlets for your spiritual life that you may find comforting as you grow in your pregnancy. For example, I found journaling, writing (obviously), and even photography to be major outlets of both release and healing.

For me, it was important to find those different forms of spirituality in my life because I became hypersensitive to people who offered to pray for me or implied that my pregnancy meant that I needed to be "saved."

> Everyone is different, and it is important to continue to follow the spiritual practices that are meaningful to you, even if it's hard at first.

As my friend Megan so aptly put it, "Once [my] pregnancy was out in the open, I was still nervous to get excited about it. I felt like it was expected for me to be ashamed." Because she wasn't married, Megan's mother was even advised by a Catholic counselor to make Megan's baby shower a "somber" occasion; she was told that "we are here as a show of support and there should be no happiness," explained Megan. "No games. No balloons. Prayers over presents."

Having an unplanned pregnancy before you're married puts you in a unique position to be judged—you are sporting your sin in the form of a prominent baby bump. We know that we are all sinners; we know that everyone makes mistakes. But the difference is, a lot of those sins can be hidden away from the public eye, buried in those deep places that we don't like to look in. Lies, secrets, addictions— these are sins that can be masked, denied, and not dealt with. But a baby belly is out there for the whole world to see—and judge. For whatever reason, there's something about seeing a young, pregnant woman, sans ring on her left hand, which spurs the "holier-than-thou" types right into action.

It's hard to struggle with the guilt and shame when you violate your personal and spiritual beliefs, and it does impact every corner of your life—I won't lie to you about that. But coming through to the other side of unplanned pregnancy, spending months in prayer, and fully experiencing peace, I can tell you that all of the judgment and the harsh words will forever change you. You will become a better and stronger person, simply because you will realize that the world is not at all what it seems. Becoming pregnant doesn't automatically make you a bad person, or a sinner in need of salvation through others. It doesn't mean you are looking for a handout or deserve public admonitions for your behavior.

Unlike a lot of adults and older, "wiser" people in the world, you will know the truth. We cannot judge the circumstances of others, nor can we predict the outcome of their lives. All we can do is offer support, love, and hope to find the good in each and every situation. As one young mom on my blog said, "It's kind of like we're being pruned. We may be upset that there are so many steps backward (like God cutting back our beautiful branches), but in the grand scheme of things, we are being made into something much greater."

CHAPTER SIX

How Does This Work? The Truth about Giving Birth (Including the Good, the Bad, and the Baby)

In all of this pesky business about dealing with an unexpected pregnancy and coming to terms with, oh, *completely changing everything about your life,* there may be one thing that slips your mind.

Giving birth.

One of the most horrifying things about getting pregnant for me, shortly after the surprise of the two tiny blue lines on the plastic stick, was the realization that *oh my gosh, this baby has to come out.*

Of me.

Call me crazy, but I was so busy trying to deal with the emotional and spiritual ramifications of my pregnancy that I kind of forgot—or more accurately, intentionally avoided—the fact that one way or another, my baby had to make his or her grand entrance into the world.

What's even more surprising is that at the time of my pregnancy, I was working as a student nurse on a labor and delivery floor. And I *still* managed to avoid thinking about the reality of having a baby. Apparently, I am a master of denial.

So if you are pregnant for the first time, you may be a bit like I was and ignoring that little thing called *labor*. Maybe you don't think it's that big of a deal. Maybe you'll be one of those women who sails through contractions and sneezes out a baby. But either way, I'm betting that you are just a little curious about what giving birth actually entails.

Not only have I given birth three times in my twenty-six years on earth so far, a fact that still manages to astound me, but after graduating from student nurse to a full-blown labor and delivery nurse today, I have had the unique opportunity to experience the "miracle of life" from both ends.

So what wisdom will I choose to impart to you from my vast knowledge of both birthing and helping to catch babies?

Yes, you might poop.

Fortunately, the fact that you might poop is not that big of a deal, nor will it be a shock to your nurses and doctor. In fact, pooping is a sign that you are pushing effectively and making way for the baby. Yay!

Okay, so now that we have the pooping issue out the way, let's break down labor and delivery, shall we?

The Birth Plan

I am a huge advocate for doing your homework and understanding all of the different choices that are available to you during childbirth. Water birth, Jacuzzi tub for labor, epidural or no epidural—it is incredibly important to educate yourself on what

> It is incredibly important to educate yourself on what your labor and delivery experience will entail, so you will be able to make informed decisions when the time comes.

your labor and delivery experience will entail, so you will be able to make informed decisions when the time comes.

That being said, I'm going to tell you, as a nurse, that the best plan is to be flexible. Every mom that I have seen with a detailed birth plan pretty much ends up with nothing that she planned on. In fact, there is a running joke amongst labor and delivery nurses that rigid birth plans always end up as C-sections—because for whatever reason, those people that want everything planned to a T are the ones that seem to get hit with every unplanned complication in the book. Think of your plan and choices as guides, because when it comes to pregnancy and giving birth, things can change in an instant.

Is It Time?

One of the hardest parts of being a first-time mom is knowing when it's time to head to the hospital. As a labor and delivery nurse, it's definitely the most common thing I see—new moms anxious and worried they are in labor, coming in to get checked out, only to be sent home.

In general, your first labor will take some time. Early labor can even stop and start and last a couple of days. And having gone through it three times, it's tempting for me to just say, *guys, trust me*, when labor is real, *you will know.* But I won't, because honest to God, I have seen an eighteen-year-old walk up to the nurses' station, chomping on her gum and texting on her phone, telling us she "like, thought she, like, might be in labor." And she was dilated to eight centimeters!

To borrow a quote from my obstetrician, "When in doubt, get it checked out." Never be embarrassed to call your care provider or head to the hospital to be evaluated.

For help in discerning if, indeed, it is *that time*, here is my quick and dirty checklist to ask yourself:

1. **Do my contractions get worse when I walk?** This is the best sign that your labor is real. If your contractions lessen or become more spaced apart when you get up and walk around, they are probably not "real" yet. In true labor, contractions will get more intense or frequent when you are standing or walking around.

2. **Are my contractions regular?** In true and active labor, contractions are spaced at regular intervals. In general, *active labor* means that contractions are every two to three minutes, but that can vary. I have seen women deliver with contractions spaced at ten minutes apart, but as a general rule of thumb, you can wait until your contractions are coming at regular intervals, even when you're up and moving.

3. **Has my water broken?** If your water has broken, there's no question of how often or how intense your contractions are—it's time to go to the hospital. Once that water is broken, there's a risk of infection. Usually, labor kicks in shortly after your water does break. Keep in mind that your water doesn't always break like it does in the movies—it can happen as a slow leak, or trickle a little. Unfortunately, if you're not sure if your water broke, the only way to know is to be evaluated, so you will need to call your doctor and possibly head to the hospital.

4. **Am I bleeding?** Although a small amount of "bloody show" (discharge that is brown or blood-tinged) is normal during early labor, if you are having any bright red bleeding, you need to be seen immediately.

Labor

If you remember one thing from this chapter, it should be this: every woman labors differently. My mother swore up and down that contractions were hard, but pushing was a relief. While I did okay with my contractions, when it came time to push, I swore I would never trust my mother again because *she was a horrible, two-faced liar.* (Love you, Mum!)

Every woman's body is different, and every woman experiences labor and delivery differently. Some women struggle with pushing; some women find pushing to be a relief. Some sail through contractions, while others are begging

> Every woman's body is different, and every woman experiences labor and delivery differently.

for an epidural before they are even dilated to one centimeter. I have seen a woman laugh while pushing her baby out and a ninety-pound woman deliver a ten-pound kid without any drugs and seemingly no pain.

The bottom line is, you can prepare for how you will handle birth (and you definitely should!), but you just can't predict how labor will feel to you. Give yourself permission to change your mind, and don't fall prey to the comparison game. You don't get a medal for giving birth without an epidural and you shouldn't feel like you "failed" if you end up with a C-section.

We are all different, but the end result is the same—a baby!

Giving Birth

The first time I saw a birth, I was in shock.

Did that seriously just come out of there? I wondered, my eyes wide as I backed out of the room in my navy blue nursing student scrubs. I'll never forget the mixture of wonder, amazement, and incredulity that I felt with that first birth, and those feelings have pretty much continued with every birth I've been privileged enough to witness.

But let's face it—birth is well, intense, to say the least. As a first-time mom, it can feel surreal when it's time to push. With my first daughter, I remember thinking, *Really? This is it? I'm not ready!*

It felt incredibly awkward to put my entire nether regions on display and start pushing. Luckily, I'll tell you that the awkwardness will soon dissipate and your body will take over. As Raquel Kato relates, "The most surprising thing about birth is how open you become. Initially, I thought I would be embarrassed having so much of myself exposed to strangers along with the common fear of pooping during birth, but all of those fears disappear when it's go-time."

So what does giving birth actually feel like? Again, it's different for every woman, but I felt all of my contraction pain in my lower abdomen and pelvis. I expected contractions to hurt throughout my entire stomach, but all of the pain was lower. Contractions were more manageable to me, but pushing was pretty painful, because it felt like bone-on-bone pain as I felt the baby's head press through my pelvis. When the baby's head crowns, there is definitely that "ring of fire" that they talk about—it's an intense burning as your skin stretches in ways you never thought possible. Unfortunately, the only way past that pain is through it, so if you have the ability to remember anything at the point, *you have to push through it.* Next, comes the incredibly strange feeling of having a head sticking out of your body, but usually the baby slithers right out and you will feel the most relief of your entire life . . . *You did it! The baby's out! She's healthy! It's over!*

And if you're wondering how your man will react to watching you give birth, Stephanie Lake's boyfriend pretty much summed it up when he said, "It was the most awesome, magical, gross, amazing thing I've ever seen!"

And there you have it.

C-section

Many women I have spoken with who have had C-sections, whether scheduled for complications during pregnancy or because of an emergency during labor, have described feeling "cheated" out of the birth experience they dreamed of or struggled with feeling like they didn't "really" give birth.

Andrea Owen, a life coach and mother of two, had a scheduled C-section with her first child. "I had a really hard time with my C-section," said Andrea. "I felt guilty for not being happy with his birth; I felt like I shouldn't complain. A healthy baby is all that matters, but I wanted permission to grieve this birth that I had always dreamed of having."

If you are scheduled for a C-section, be sure to talk with your doctor or midwife about some ways you can incorporate immediate skin-to-skin contact with your baby or make it more family oriented to help ease the transition. But most of all, if you do experience a C-section, remember that the health of you and your baby is all that matters. Families aren't born just by birth alone!

The Aftermath

One of the most astonishing things to occur when you have a baby is the cleanup. Labor and delivery nurses are awesome for this, because in twenty minutes, you can go from pushing in stirrups for all the world to see, to neat and tidy with a fresh gown and a clean baby in your arms. And maybe even a vase full of flowers to boot.

But there still will be some major cleanup down there that you will have to go through. You will be bleeding after birth and perched up on some highly absorbent pads that some people like to call "puppy pads." Yes, it's really as glamorous as it sounds.

Your nurse will have to check your belly and rub on your uterus to make sure it's closing properly, and that is really uncomfortable, but it is necessary, so try not to swat her hand away, as much as you would like to.

And then, it will be time.

To get up and go to the bathroom.

If you didn't have an epidural, you can get up and go to the bathroom almost right away. If you had the epidural, you will of course have to wait until your legs "thaw out." Do not, I repeat, do not, attempt to get out of bed without your nurse's help. You will need it, plus there's always the fun chance that you could pass out.

When you do get up to go to the bathroom for the first time, be prepared—there will be a *lot* of blood. You aren't dying; I promise. But going from lying in bed to standing up and walking has the effect of causing all that pooled blood to make a quick getaway. Just take it slowly and follow your nurse's instructions to keep the mess to a minimum.

It will be scary to use the facilities for the first time after the trauma you have just been through, so try to relax and use the little squeeze bottle to ease the burn, especially if you have an episiotomy. And load up on those witch hazel pads they give you—they will be a lifesaver. Make sure you pack extra in your bag, and feign innocence when your nurse wonders where the three she just gave you went.

The Best Meal of Your Life

Yes, a whole section is devoted to this subject, because your first meal after giving birth will be the best meal of your life. I have come to the conclusion that giving birth burns approximately one million calories, and I want you to enjoy *each and every one of them* after you have that baby.

You thought you were hungry when you were pregnant? Please. You haven't seen anything yet. So put all those well-meaning visitors to use and don't be afraid to ask people to bring you food.

For instance, here's a sample post-delivery meal for me, almost verbatim of what I enjoyed after having both of my daughters.

- One Bennigan's "Big Irish" Burger, complete with bacon, cheese, fried onions, and a Guinness beer glaze

- One side of steamed broccoli (I happen to love broccoli, so it's just a fluke that it's healthy.)

- One sugar cookie

- One piece of strawberry-smothered cheesecake

This almost makes me want to have another baby, just so I can eat like this again.

Although it may be hard to start thinking about the reality of your life with a baby or the reality of delivering your baby, I promise that it really will be all right. One of the most beautiful things about giving birth and becoming a mother is that the strength of the millions of women who have come before you will surround and empower you. You are now a part of something bigger, better, and truly amazing. You are literally an instrument in creation, and God's plan for you and your baby is just starting to unfold.

So cheers to the best meal—and day—of your life!

CHAPTER SEVEN

Who Am I Now? How to Reclaim Your Life

I don't know how to tell you this, but I have something to confess.

I haven't always loved my baby.

Allow me to explain.

For me, the hardest part of my unplanned pregnancy was the emotional acceptance. I knew that I could *physically* care for a baby—I was raised in a large family in which babies abounded; I worked in obstetrics, so I knew how to change diapers and swaddle. What I didn't know was how to accept that I was a mother at the age of twenty-one.

I definitely was not one of those women who spent hours researching baby names or comparing the baby's size to various tropical fruits (who really knows how big a rutabaga is, anyway?) or forcing headphones playing Mozart onto their baby bumps. I was terrified of my baby. Instead of facing what was happening, I kept myself busy—I had a full class schedule and nursing clinicals, I ran a student organization (which, coincidentally was a group devoted to student *parents*—oh, the irony!), and I worked nights at the hospital. I avoided any fetal development information. I didn't want to know what was going on in there, because frankly I was too scared to even contemplate the reality that I was going to be a mother.

I felt like a freak of nature. Where was my rosy glow of motherly love pictured on the covers of the *What to Expect When You're Expecting* books? Definitely not here.

I felt no maternal rush of love during my pregnancy. No attachment to the little person taking up residence on my bladder. Nothing.

In case you haven't already figured it out, this chapter is not exactly a mushy-gushy ode to your baby and the "miracle of life." This chapter is about *your* new life and the reality of adjusting to it. For me, the fact that my pregnancy caused my entire life plan to shift was really hard to grasp. I had a plan for how I wanted things to go in my life, and the pregnancy shook everything up.

While I was busy avoiding my pregnancy, I sunk into a kind of pre-partum depression. I shut down. I didn't imagine what my baby would look like. I didn't rub my belly and talk to her. I

> I had a plan for how I wanted things to go in my life, and the pregnancy shook everything up.

just put my head down and kept moving. If I worked enough and studied hard enough, I didn't have to stop to think about how much my life was actually changing. I completely gave up on my goals, dreams, and any plans for the future.

The truth is, I didn't let myself bond with my baby. Looking back, of course, it seems crazy, but at the time, there were a few contributing factors in my struggle:

1. I didn't feel like I deserved be happy about having a baby.

2. I didn't know if I *was* happy about having a baby.

3. I was really, really afraid that I would be a bad mother.

4. The fact that I wasn't bonding with my baby seemed like pretty good proof that I was already a bad mother.

I wasn't alone in my difficulty bonding with my baby. When I asked my cousin Mandy if she bonded with her son Brady before he was actually born, she admitted, "This is tough to say, but not really. I was mostly determined to ignore my pregnancy as much as possible during my first and second trimester. Once I started getting used to being pregnant, I was more comfortable with my baby. It sounds bad, but it's almost as if I had to get permission to be happy about being pregnant. I guess I had to get permission from myself, which took a while."

Writer Michelle Horton of the online community *Early Mama* found that although she was doing all the right things—stocking up on baby goods, eating right and exercising, even talking to her baby while she drove in the car—she still wasn't bonding. "I fooled myself into believing I was bonding with Noah," Michelle said. "I genuinely cared for him. But I was in such a state of perpetual disbelief and denial that it was like I was just going through the motions. I was bonding with a pregnancy, but not my baby. I knew I had to take care of whatever was growing inside me, but I was truly shocked when a baby came out of me."

Taylor Shelton, a blogger and young mom, didn't bond with either of her babies—both unplanned, although she was married. "I was too scared to be excited!" she said.

And Kayla McAfee, an aspiring artist who discovered she was pregnant while traveling alone in Germany, knows exactly what I felt like in thinking I didn't deserve to bond with my baby. "I really had a hard time allowing myself to enjoy and bond with my baby during the pregnancy because I felt guilty," Kayla wrote to me in an e-mail. "As if the baby was a punishment for bad behavior and I should treat it that way."

You may be expecting me to tell you there was an "aha" moment when I fell in love with my baby, but it didn't happen. I didn't experience a single bonding moment with my baby during my entire pregnancy. I have a vivid memory of myself shortly before I gave birth sitting at a Chinese restau-

> I didn't experience a single bonding moment with my baby during my entire pregnancy.

rant with my in-laws. Protesting the nauseating sweet-and-sour chicken I had just consumed, my baby developed a major case of the hiccups. As Ben's sister and I watched my belly jerk up and down with every hiccup, all I could think about was how incredibly and terrifyingly unreal it all was. I was this enormous creature, sitting in a dimly lit restaurant with awful, wilting Chinese food . . . and somehow I was supposed to become not just a pregnant person, but an actual, real, live mother? How did this happen? Where did my life go?

A few days later, I wasn't doing much better. Alone at home one night, having just celebrated my twenty-second birthday and my college graduation, watching the sun set from the balcony of our tiny apartment, I started to panic. My husband was at work. My life was gone. I didn't love my baby. I wouldn't be a good mother. Classes had ended, the nursery was set up, and I had folded the last receiving blanket. There was nothing left to do, nothing left to distract myself from the fear I had about becoming a mother.

I crept silently into the small spare bedroom that served as the nursery, painted a pale, yet cheerful yellow for the baby we had yet to know was a girl. My eyes swept over the wooden crib, handmade by my husband, the rocking chair he had built before we found out we were even pregnant, the white wicker hand-me-down shelving housing the few toys and books we had purchased.

And suddenly, I was angry. Angry that this was happening. Angry that everything was completely and utterly out of my control. Angry that I had to give birth. Angry that I didn't know what the future would hold.

And so I did what any rational human being about to become a mother would do. I tore apart the nursery, overturning the little rocking horse that a great-aunt had shipped over. I flung toys off the shelves and threw them in the middle of the room I had vacuumed just a few hours earlier. I tore through the closet, flinging blankets and burp cloths that I had so carefully ironed that morning over my head. I cried and screamed hysterically, threw over the bassinet, and finally locked myself in my closet to cry.

I didn't ask for this! I screamed in my head. *I can't do this.*

I cried and screamed at my empty apartment, hot, angry tears falling as I pounded my head against the wall next to my closet.

And when at last I collapsed, exhausted and spent, into the same position as that first fateful night when I had taken my pregnancy test, my husband found me and wondered, I'm sure, just when exactly his calm, absurdly pregnant wife had been replaced by a raving lunatic. But he said nothing.

Because, really, what was there to say?

Instead, he wisely kissed me silently on the forehead and tucked me into bed for one of the last full nights of sleep I would have in a long time.

The next morning, I found that my rage and fear and panic had been replaced by a strange sense of calm. I wasn't exactly peaceful, but I was resigned. In the bright sunlight that filtered in through the windows, I refolded the baby blankets and burp clothes and righted the rocking horse. I returned the bassinet to its proper place and lovingly tucked the teeny mattress inside of it.

And waited.

Those last few weeks of pregnancy are so intense, and yet also painfully agonizing in uneventful waiting. You feel like time stretches out in an eternity before you, so much to contemplate, and yet, too much to even start to think about. There's the pain of labor, the wonder of what giving birth will be like, the sheer enormity of the fact that you will go into the hospital with a belly and come out with a baby.

I waited some more. In the meantime, I may have eaten a donut or two. Or four.

Finally, I woke up one morning a week before my due date to discover that my water was leaking. It wasn't a lot, mind you; just enough to make me question if I had, in fact, lost all control of my bladder and was destined to be one of those moms constantly sneezing and crossing her legs or avoiding trampolines at all costs, but I called my midwife anyway. Because I lived almost two hours away from the hospital, she told me to wait a while, go for a walk, and see if my contractions kicked in.

So we walked, my girl and I. Although, of course, I didn't know she was a girl at the time. But we walked anyway—up and down our back dirt road, getting lost in the woods and wandering down to the stream. I must have walked more than seven miles that day. And even though all that walking did zilch for me on the contraction scale, I needed that time to make peace with my pregnancy and embrace the new person I was to become.

I'll never forget that day; I perched my very pregnant self upon a flat, mossy rock overlooking the water and had a serious heart-to-heart with the little person I had inadvertently created inside of me. I hid myself as best I could, in case anyone happened to walk by and wonder who the crazy pregnant lady crouching in the bushes was.

I poured my heart out to my baby, apologizing to her for being so scared and promising her that I would do my best to be a good mom. I admitted to her that I really didn't have a clue what I was doing, but I hoped she would love me anyway. I told her that I wanted to always be in her life, through tantrums and turbulent teen years and someday when we could be old together and drink coffee at my kitchen table. I asked her if she could forgive me for her somewhat chaotic entry into the world, and if she wouldn't mind giving her mama an easy labor.

But most of all, I told her I was ready. I was ready to become her mom.

She must have believed me, because I went into labor later that night. We made the long trek to the hospital with me cursing each and every bump and pothole in the road and arrived just after midnight.

And after nine months of wondering if I would be the world's worst mother for not loving my own offspring, sixteen hours of all-natural labor, and an exhausting three hours of pushing, I finally met my daughter.

In that moment, when the midwife placed my daughter on my chest, I was filled with wonder, relief, and joy as the purest, most overwhelming rush of love washed over me.

I looked down at her, awed and amazed that she was actually real and had somehow materialized from inside of my body, and my first thought was simply this:

Oh, there you are.

Instantly, it seemed laughable that I had worried about loving her. I felt, in gazing at her for the first time, such sweet relief in the recognition of my heart to her. I felt like I had always known her, my daughter, and that she had always been mine. I looked at her, feeling a love so all-encompassing that it didn't seem real, and knew, finally, what it meant to become a mother.

We chose the name Ada for our daughter, a name of Hebrew origin that means, "beautiful one; treasured daughter; a woman's preciousness and beauty."

I love my daughter's name, because not only is she truly precious, but because it reminds me of how her birth brought forward the beauty of being a woman and a mother to me. I didn't have to be afraid of loving her anymore. She was my daughter, my treasured daughter, and I knew I would love her forever.

In that moment, when I fully embraced being a mother, my heart recognized that from now on, I would forever be transformed. For me, the roles of motherhood and selfhood have become closely intertwined. I imagine one of those trees, made up of separate twisting, turning vines that cross and circle each other until they make up one whole, slightly awkward, perfect tree. And within that tree, weaving in and out, are the indelible impressions that motherhood made on my soul.

I felt them quietly at first, as a whisper of a thought, an idea, a dream I dared not follow. Somewhere in that hazy time after Ada was born, they rose up like a little flutter of hope in the empty space of me, the space she had left behind. Holding Ada close, her eyes intent on my face, rocking away hours with the moonlight outside my window, I heard them. *Be the mother you always wanted to be. Show your daughter that it doesn't end here. Make her proud.*

I have finally found my way in life, because I have found my passion—and it was born that day at exactly 4:51 p.m.

In the end, I have realized that motherhood has not taken away my sense of self—it has only transformed it. The key to motherhood is realizing that I am now made up of fluid boundaries; instead of fighting to keep separate my "mom" and "non-mom" roles, I let them move in and out of each other, interchanging and shifting, like a shimmering, permeable membrane. And while this may sound like a beautiful and noble act, sometimes it's as simple as stopping in the middle of an essay to change the baby's diaper or putting off a phone call until the kids are tucked away safely at nap time. But other times, it's the awe-inspiring realization that motherhood—this permeable membrane—has also given me everything I ever dreamed about. The very thing I feared most has actually become the key to unlocking all my heart's desires.

> In the end, I have realized that motherhood has not taken away my sense of self—it has only transformed it.

I am so in awe of all that motherhood has given me. And while I won't claim to be a glowing oracle of happiness on motherhood at all hours of the day and night (it's much easier to sing the praises of motherhood while I'm tucked away in my office, listening to the rain on my window and drinking hazelnut coffee while the kids are all sleeping), I feel that I have finally made peace with what it means to be a mother. I sit in silent reverence at the throne of motherhood, never doubting again where it will take me in life.

If you are experiencing any trouble bonding with your baby during your pregnancy and doubting if you will ever love your baby, please allow me to assure you—you will. It will happen. It may not happen right when your baby is born (strangely enough, I didn't bond as quickly with my "planned" children; it took days for me to fully bond with my son—and he was my third child!), but it *will* happen.

I know many of you will be afraid that you aren't good enough, old enough, mature enough, rich enough, or ready enough to become a mother, but believe me when I say:

You are all that your baby needs.

You—as a mother—are enough.

Your love will be enough.

It already is enough.

CHAPTER EIGHT

What Did She Just Say? How to Deal with Rude People

I stood in the back of the church, a new mom proudly holding my baby girl to my chest. I watched as the people in line for communion filed back to their seats, a steady stream of families, parents, and couples.

One elderly woman shuffled past her pew and headed toward the back of the church, her eyes fastened intently on me. I smiled at her, anticipating the coos and praises over my sweet baby that every mom loves to hear.

Instead, she gripped Ada's bare feet violently with wrinkly hands, spotted and topped with razor-like fingernails.

"How dare you leave her uncovered!" she spat at me, her words shocking me with their fierce, unveiled contempt. "This poor little baby is freezing!"

My friends, it was the middle of June and I had dressed Ada in her first adorable little sundress. Her feet dangled bare from my arms and I swear to you, she was sweating.

As a young mom, you will have to deal with rude people. It's practically a law. If I had a dollar for every time someone asked me how old I was or muttered a "babies-having-babies" comment under his or her breath, you had

> As a young mom, you will have to deal with rude people.

better believe I'd be stockpiling diapers like they were going out of style. In the beginning with Ada, I took offense to the rude treatment, primarily because I felt like every comment on my young age was a direct judgment on my abilities as a mother.

I'll never forget the first speech I ever gave after I started publicly speaking out for young moms. I was so nervous about getting up in front of what I knew was a really conservative audience and sharing my "sin" with them, but I knew that what I had to say was important. I knew that I needed to speak out against the judgment of young moms, so I invited my whole family to come and proudly dressed Ada up in a little dress for her big debut.

After the speech, I sat down and my mom handed Ada to me. I sat with her in my lap, my cheeks flushed with excitement as I listened to the moderator delivering his closing remarks for the evening.

"I just want to say one thing," he started as my post-speech glow began to fade and my stomach started to drop. "I'm glad that Chaunie and her daughter are here and that she made the choice that she did—but I want to be clear and say that we don't support the choices she made that led her to getting pregnant. I have a daughter at college and that is not behavior that I approve of. We need to be extra vigilant when it comes to talking about this, because we don't want—I wouldn't want my daughter—ending up in this situation."

Talk about humiliating. I ran out of the room sobbing, my heart breaking at the thought that this man felt the need to offer a disclaimer against me to the entire room; my worst fear had come true. Since that night, not one speech has passed without a similar rude and judgmental comment. Just a few days ago, after a speech I did locally, a man came up to me afterward with a book and said, "I think you really need to read this." It was a book titled *Hell Is For Real*.

People think that it's acceptable to judge young moms; we are defined for one choice that we made, and it's not usually the one we made to continue our pregnancy. If you haven't yet experienced this particular brand of fun as a young mom, just wait till you take your first trip out with your baby. There will be not-so-inconspicuous looks at your ring finger; other mothers looking you up and down; and people in every office who will assume your brain has fallen out of the birth canal along with the baby. There's just something about being a young mom that signals to the outside world that you are an unintelligent human being.

"I didn't have many people openly say anything to me, but if looks could kill, I would be dead," writes my unplanned-pregnancy soul sister Raquel Kato, a fellow Catholic mom who found out she was pregnant her senior year of college. "People stare. I'm pretty sure I was the only pregnant girl on my college campus, so I got a lot of looks. For an already broken, very self-conscious girl, having dozens of people looking at you constantly is not enjoyable. People were awkward around me. It was as if I was an elephant in the room (almost literally by my third trimester)."

Simple shopping trips often have the tendency to turn into young-mom judging fests. Like the one a pregnant Paula Rollo, a blogger at the website BeautyThroughImperfection.com, encountered when shopping at Target with her eighteen-month-old in tow. "This woman had been slowly walking around on the phone in front of us and I had finally gotten past her," writes Paula. "We were moving on through the store, minding our own business, when the same lady puts her phone on hold and comes running after me, yelling at me and begins telling me I *can't* let my son do something and I *must* make him stop. (She didn't like the way he was in the cart, though he was completely safe.) I got away from her, but I ended up crying when I got to my car. I had never been treated so rudely. This woman made a major scene just to tell me what a terrible job I was doing with my son."

One of my personal favorite rude comments is when people think they have the right to ask you if the baby was planned or not—as if that makes a difference? My cousin Mandy was minding her own business one afternoon, doing some grocery shopping after a particularly trying day with her infant son.

"Oh, you look tired," commented the grocery clerk sympathetically. "Were you at work?"

Mandy stared her down. "Taking care of the baby, yeah," she replied, running her grocery list over in her head. *Did the two for three count for that frozen broccoli?*

The clerk nodded. "Oh, I see. So, was he planned?"

Smooth, right? I have to hand it to this particular grocery clerk for the most ridiculous rude comment transition ever. Not only did she manage to insult Mandy for not working a "real" job, but she also managed to insinuate that Mandy was a deadbeat mom. As unbelievable as the clerk's question was, Mandy owned this situation. "Brady is here now," she wrote on her blog. "It doesn't matter to me where he came from—planned or unplanned, adopted or conceived—nothing could impact how much I love him. And though it might make some good gossip or an interesting twist on a television show, the fact that I got pregnant my senior year of college doesn't really concern anyone else. And it's not something I am willing to guilt myself about anymore." So Mandy smiled at the cashier that day and said simply, "He was a surprise. A very handsome one."

Taylor Shelton, a married young mom of two, is no stranger to rude treatment. "From the time I began sporting my baby bump, I got a lot of, 'But you're just a baby!' comments," she told me. "And to this day, strangers indirectly say things like, "Your parents are still babies!" to our daughter.

Even my sister-in-law, who was a married woman when she became a mom at the age of twenty-one, admits that she had trouble announcing her pregnancy. "I actually felt embarrassed to tell people," she said. "Because I wasn't 'supposed' to get pregnant so soon. Everyone wanted to tell me how hard it would be."

What is it about being a young mom that makes people think they can say whatever they want to you? Do our bellies display signs that read, "Please ridicule me. I'm asking for it because I'm young and pregnant, so I must be stupid?" I don't get it. I feel like people honestly think that we "deserve" a little talking-to because we have so clearly gone astray off the beaten path.

> What is it about being a young mom that makes people think they can say whatever they want to you?

Yes, there are some questionable young mothers out there—but they exist at every age. As young-mom Jeanne Sanger says, "I know some young moms who absolutely suck at the job. I know some old moms who really stink. And then I know women of both age groups who are fantastic mothers. I think we moms need to be nicer both to each other and to ourselves. I spent a lot of time when my daughter was younger beating myself up for every little mistake I made, but I look at my amazing, quirky, whip-smart little girl now. She's the person she is because of what I did right and what I did wrong."

I would never criticize another mother's parenting or publicly belittle her. I know passing a mom with a screaming kid at the store or a little one misbehaving in church doesn't tell me anything about that mom—those passing moments are snippets, not the whole picture of someone else's life or anything that we can or should base judgments on. And yet, sometimes it feels like others don't pay young moms the same courtesy.

Take Miranda Gonzales, for example, a new wife who purposefully chose young motherhood. While shopping at Sam's Club, sporting her newly showing baby bump, Miranda was shocked when an elderly woman commented out loud, "Anyone can have children these days at any age. You need a license to drive a car, but not to have a kid."

Emily, a teen mom and current student parent, says, "I think as a young mom, so many assumptions get made, and everybody is so quick to judge you—even strangers. The number of disapproving looks I get in public still to this day astounds me. People will look and see that I'm young, and it is almost like they automatically think they *know* what type of mom I am. Obviously, people have been watching too much *Teen Mom*. But I hate feeling stereotyped because I had a child at a young age. I work very hard to break the mold of what people expect from teenage mothers."

One of my favorite stories about how people treat young moms comes from a fellow young mom of three, twenty-seven-year-old Hannah Wingert, who runs an online children's boutique.

"I look really young," explains Hannah. "So a lot of people assume that I'm a teen mom. Before I had three kids, I used to get a lot of pitying or dirty looks and would usually try to flash my wedding ring at them so they'd see that I was at least married. Then, when my oldest daughter was still a baby, I lost my wedding ring. The looks and comments got even worse after that. When my daughter was four months old, she had to have an ultrasound to check for hip dysplasia. My husband was working, and I was nervous about navigating the Mayo Clinic by myself, so I asked my mom to come with me. I can't tell you how many people assumed that she was the mom and I was the older sister. During the ultrasound, my daughter started crying, so I tried to comfort her. The ultrasound tech looked at me condescendingly and said, 'Oh, what a good mom you are.' I could tell she thought I was a teen mom and that my mom was virtually raising the baby for me. It was humiliating. And then, just last month, I took my youngest daughter to the doctor to have her frenulum clipped, and I asked my mom to come along for moral support. I left the older two kids with my sister, so it was just me, my mom, and the baby. While in the office, the nurse would look at my mom instead of me when asking questions. She was nice, but she obviously thought I was too young to have a baby. When she left the office, I struck up a conversation with my mom about how so many people think I'm too young to have a baby even though I'm twenty-seven and married with three kids. The nurse was standing right outside and must have heard, because after that, she directed her questions to me!"

Sometimes, the judgment lies in what people *don't* say. "The phrase, 'You're so young' really means, 'You are way too young to be a mother; you must have been irresponsible and gotten knocked up,'" explains Raquel Kato. "I remember a classmate asked me what I was having. When I told him she was a girl, he said, 'Dang, why didn't you get an abortion?' I remember being so shocked that anyone would ever say such a horrible thing that I couldn't even reply."

One of the hardest parts about being judged as a young mom for me was the stereotype that surrounded using government resources. As a pregnant student attending school full time, running a student organization, and working part time, I did try to use some of the government resources that exist to help low-income, pregnant women and parents. For instance, after Ben and I got married, I was no longer eligible to use my parents' insurance, and the student insurance at my school specifically excluded maternity coverage. With no other options as a full-time student, I turned to Medicaid, which is something that I instantly felt ashamed for using.

I also qualified for the Women, Infants, and Children (WIC) program, which provides low-income mothers with coupons for food. I decided to give the WIC program a shot to ensure that every dollar I saved could go toward supporting my baby. I was terrified to use WIC because I was afraid of being judged and treated like I was ignorant; I had heard many horror stories about using WIC, including from my own mother, who had used WIC when she went back to school for her teaching license while my brother and I were still toddlers. She was an educated woman with a bachelor's degree in mathematics, and yet the WIC officer insisted that she physically demonstrate that she knew how to brush her teeth.

I thought times had surely changed since my mother had used WIC, so I went to the office, determined not to let other people's judgment bother me. After all, I was mere months away from graduating with my bachelor's degree in nursing. Surely, they could see that I was not the "typical" young mom, right?

Um, no. I was humiliated along with everyone else. They talked slowly to me, often sighing in irritation when I asked a question and insisted on going over every aspect of the food pyramid with me. As if I hadn't studied it from top to bottom in my nursing program already. It felt like it didn't matter—I was a young mom on government aid, and therefore I was worthless and ignorant.

I tried to convince myself that it didn't matter—I knew the truth—that I was an educated, intelligent woman, and that it was acceptable to use some help to get me through to graduation. Until the day that a war was launched against me in the grocery store checkout lane. That day, I chose the express lane in the supermarket and used a WIC coupon to purchase some cereal. However, unbeknownst to me, I had grabbed the wrong brand of cereal. WIC only covers certain kinds of cereal and, in my eagerness to slow down the incredible growing phenomenon formerly known as my body, I had chosen the "healthier" *whole-wheat* Chex. WIC, apparently, covers only Corn Chex and Rice Chex.

While I was unsuspectingly browsing the gossip magazines, a war was being waged against me. The cashier spotted my whole-wheat Chex. Saw my hugely conspicuous WIC coupon, separated items of my order (another indignity of WIC—they make it *so* obvious), looked down on my very pregnant belly, and suddenly, her eyes narrowed as she put it all together. She waved over her fellow cashier from the next aisle. Together they huddled, whispering about me and shooting looks over their shoulders as they decided on my fate.

As the line grew behind me and impatient foot-tapping filled the air, my eyes welled with tears and my face burned red. I heard the voices of what all the customers behind me were thinking in my mind. *Stupid girl. She didn't know better than to not get pregnant; now she doesn't even know how to buy cereal!*

The two cashiers, emboldened by their strength in numbers, dealt the first blow. Cashier A, who happened to be missing her two front teeth, sneered, "You can't get this kind of cereal!"

Cashier B backed her condemning mate up.

"How could you not know that?" she said, her 1980s-era iron-sprayed hair barely moving as she shook her head and crossed her arms at me.

Shaking with humiliation, my eyes burning and cheeks flaming, I mumbled something along the lines of, "Sorry, can you just take that box off my order . . . ?"

The cashier twins rolled their eyes in disgust. Sighing with exasperation, they snatched the offending box off the conveyor belt. I handed over my WIC coupons to pay that portion of my order and swiped my credit card for the rest.

When I finally managed to escape from the store, I burst into tears and cried all the way home. I vowed that I would never, ever use WIC again. It just didn't feel worth it to risk public humiliation for some free peanut butter and eggs.

For young women, it can feel like choosing to continue an unplanned pregnancy is a no-win situation. Not only are we looked down upon for having unplanned pregnancies, but we are also judged for continuing the pregnancy and for using the few resources that are available to help us. I mean, let's be honest—an abortion would have cost a lot less than the governmental aid I received during my pregnancy. But does the fact that I chose to have my baby mean I deserved to be publicly humiliated over a box of cereal?

> For young women, it can feel like choosing to continue an unplanned pregnancy is a no-win situation.

I know that there are differing opinions about young mothers using government resources; I know this because I have been privy to many people telling me how they felt about me using government resources. After one speech that I gave, I had a lady come up to me, shaking her fist in my face and berating me:

"I do not pay taxes so that you can have fun with your boyfriend!"

I won't lie. It's hard. It was hard for me to turn to governmental aid for help, and it was hard dealing with being treated so badly for using that help—even though rationally I knew I would be "paying back" into the system in a few short months. I felt stuck and out of options, especially when it came to health insurance. I mean, there wasn't even an option to *purchase* student health insurance that would cover my pregnancy. It was either stay single and on my parents' insurance or get married and get kicked off.

In some cases, just pregnancy alone can be enough to get you kicked off your parents' insurance, a fact that Sarah Tierney of *The Mom Life* blog knows all too well. Although she was single and still living at home, she was kicked off her parents' insurance when she became pregnant at the age of seventeen.

Visiting the doctor was always a source of anxiety for me, too. I was embarrassed to flash my Medicaid card at the doctor's office, and I can still remember the first time I used a "real" insurance card after Ben started working as a teacher. I held out our shiny new insurance card proudly and asked the clerk twice if she had all our information updated—I didn't want to risk the nasty looks and feelings of guilt anymore.

Mandy Lange also faced judgment at her doctor's office during her pregnancy. "The doctor's office really made me feel that as a young mother, I had no idea what was going on," Mandy said. "A doctor actually argued with me about what I was feeling! I just know that if someone my mom's age had been describing my symptoms, the doctor wouldn't have dare corrected her."

While raising two little ones and going back to school to become a nurse, Lianne Cole, a reader of my blog, relied on some government aid to get through. "I was on WIC at one point, and I felt the shame of needing a little extra help," Lianne told me. "And yes, the grocery store lady still gives me the stink eye when I roll through with all the kids; it's even better when I forget to wear my wedding ring!"

I did feel guilty for using governmental resources, but I will always be grateful that those resources existed for me when I needed them. I landed in the hospital twice after I had Ada with postpartum complications (kidney infection and mastitis), and my stay extended over several days and included some very expensive antibiotics. When the statements came in the mail, the bill topped over ten thousand dollars. I cried and cried until I realized that—miracle of miracles—Medicaid had fully covered the expenses. I will never forget the relief I felt when I realized that because of Medicaid, my little family wouldn't be starting life out in debt. I will also never forget the fear that I felt in being uninsured; I went back to work when Ada was exactly six weeks old and paid out-of-pocket for insurance for almost two years until Ben took on a full-time job.

If you are using government resources and encountering judgment or belittlement for needing a little extra help right now, try to think of the temporary assistance as an investment. Programs like Medicaid and WIC exist to help struggling mothers with young children precisely because it is a hard time in our lives—it's hard to spend the necessary time it takes to care for young children and work and go to school.

> If you are using government resources and encountering judgment or belittlement for needing a little extra help right now, try to think of the temporary assistance as an investment.

Utilizing resources that you need to ensure your family's health and safety is an investment in your future, your children's futures, and society's future. If you need to use WIC so that you have enough money to afford child care or pay for your books to go to school, then by all means, do it! Your education is worth more than a few judgmental comments or stares.

It won't always be easy. Feeling judged for something so everyday as going to the store or to the doctor's office is a ridiculous price to pay for choosing to continue our pregnancies as young mothers.

So what's the best way to handle the rude comments, stares, and constant judgment from others? "I wish I could say I always had a witty remark and laughed it off," says Mandy, "But I just ended up getting really good at dirty looks. There comes a time, however, when you build up enough self-confidence to just roll your eyes and smile. And now? One look at Brady, and I don't even remember the rudeness. It's worth all the 'You-look-a-little-young-to-be-a-mom' comments and false assumptions of my morality just to be his mother and primary snuggle-buddy."

When you encounter the inevitable "How old are you?" questions of your own, or face rude comments simply based on your age, I want you to be able to laugh them off. Embrace it. I still get asked at the grocery store, when I have all three kiddos with me, if I will be using WIC coupons. In the beginning, I was so offended—why would they ask me that? Is it because I look young? Do my kids look dirty? Do I look like a horrible mother?

> When you encounter the inevitable "How old are you?" questions of your own, or face rude comments simply based on your age, I want you to be able to laugh them off. Embrace it.

But eventually, I got to the point where I could stand up for myself. I am a good mother, my kids are well behaved and clean (most of the time), and I don't need validation about my mothering skills from a grocery store clerk.

So I shook things up a little. One day, when the clerk asked me if I would be using WIC, I stopped and stared her in the face, baby on my hip and all.

"No, I'm not. Why would you ask me that?" I retorted coolly.

Her face immediately turned bright red. "Oh, no, I don't know . . ." she stammered.

I turned my back on her and finished loading up my groceries, feeling like I had just won a small victory.

Be proud of you who are as a young mom—you have strengths and abilities that other moms don't have. You are a good mother, and you are doing your best with what you have right now. We all need help sometimes, and for some strange reason, the world is set up to look down on young moms with kids, as if they have done something wrong, when really, they're kind of what makes the world go 'round. Am I right?

The real key in facing the judgment is learning to have confidence in yourself as a mother. In the beginning, the comments hurt me so badly precisely because I was afraid that they were right—maybe I was a bad mother.

Jessica Watson understands that feeling. She got an early start to motherhood when she became pregnant during her senior year of high school. Her daughter Ashlyn is now a teenager, but she told me, "Sometimes I think I still [have to work to overcome the stereotypes of young moms]. I remember when Ashlyn was young and began school, I never felt like I fit in with the moms, and I'm not sure I ever have. Over the years I became more and more confident in my role as her mom and I began to care less about what others thought. I still dread the 'You're her mom?' and the 'You two must be sisters' comments, but I don't take them personally in the same way that I used to."

"Find a few people you trust to give you advice when you need it and ignore everyone else. Don't let other people's opinions make you feel like you are failing."

Paula Rollo advises her fellow young moms to look past the haters. "Find a few people you trust to give you advice when you need it and ignore everyone else. Don't let other people's opinions make you feel like you are failing."

And if you are just feeling as if you have no energy or fight left in you, Raquel Kato found that sometimes, the best policy is to choose to ignore rude people. "I wish I had the guts to just tell someone off once in a while," Raquel wrote me. "But the best thing to do is ignore them."

Or, you could go with the route that teen mom Gloria Malone is often tempted to take. "Sometimes I lie to make the rude women think I'm thirty!" she laughs. But overall, she has found to best way to deal with rude people questioning her mothering is simple. "Show up, believe in yourself, and walk, talk, and act with conviction and confidence," she says.

Trust in yourself—you are a good mother. If you love your baby, and I know you do, then you are doing a good job. That's honestly all that matters.

So the next time someone makes a comment about how young you look, turn the tables, toss your hair, and flaunt it. Sometimes I wonder if some of the harsh reactions we encounter are related to the fact that people realize just how hard parenting is. And the fact that we, as young mothers, can still manage to pull it off successfully, while going to school and working and cultivating a full life, can be a lot for people to take in. They may even be projecting some of their insecurities on us—as in, if we can have it so together as young moms, why can't they? Because in the eternal motherhood paradox, we all know that we think other mothers are doing a better job than we are.

And let's admit it—deep down, they are probably just jealous that you look so good.

CHAPTER NINE

Is There a Syllabus for Parenthood? Being a Student and a Mom

~~~~~~~~~~~~~~~~~~~~~~~~~~~~~~~~~~~~~~

Although they don't always go hand in hand, an unexpected pregnancy at a young age can often mean that life as a student parent is also on the horizon.

I spent the majority of my senior year of college pregnant. I delivered Ada exactly one week after my graduation, so I avoided a lot of the difficulties that many student parents encounter. I've often said that we planned our unplanned pregnancy pretty well. (Ha!) That being said, Ben still had an entire semester to go, and I went back to school when Ada was just shy of a year old, so life as a student parent is not unfamiliar territory to me.

Having experienced life both as a pregnant student and life as a student parent, I have to say that for me, one of the hardest parts about being a pregnant student wasn't in the physical challenge of keeping my breakfast down during class, navigating an icy campus with a giant belly, or staying awake long enough to do my homework; it was in feeling so completely alone.

"I'm pretty sure I was the only pregnant girl on my college campus," confides Raquel Kato, twenty-one-year-old mom of Ava. She goes on to say,

The hardest part about being a student parent is that you have completely different priorities from the other students. In general, college is about finding 'yourself' and doing what 'you' want to do. The life of a mom is all about your baby and tending to her around the clock. Of course it's good to take time for yourself, but your baby is such a huge priority, if not your first priority. Because of that responsibility, motherhood doesn't exactly mesh with the typical college lifestyle. You can't just spontaneously hang out with friends, go out to the bars, sleep in, or even procrastinate on homework. On the bright side, while everyone is complaining about pulling all-nighters for finals week, you have way more confidence in performing with little sleep because you've been waking up every three hours at night for the past several months!

In one of the great ironies of life, I had actually spent the entire summer before I became pregnant interning with an organization called Feminists for Life and working on their college outreach program—basically an entire program built and designed to help pregnant and parenting students on campus. I loved the mission and was so inspired by all the work being done to help pregnant women in college. So when I became pregnant, you can believe that I knew that I had to use my experience to help other women like me on campus.

Changing Campus

Remember the story of how I paid my campus health center a little visit for a confirmation pregnancy test? And the nurse left me crying and alone in her office?

Well, after that fun and encouraging visit, things kind of went downhill. After I had made the decision to go through with my pregnancy and finish college, I wanted to know everything—and I mean *everything*—there was to know about being a pregnant student on campus.

Unfortunately, it took me a remarkably short amount of time to learn everything, because there wasn't a lot to learn. There wasn't a whole lot in terms of resources and support on my college campus for pregnant and parenting students. I started with health insurance. As I mentioned earlier, my school did offer student insurance for purchase, but for some reason, every single plan specifically excluded maternity coverage.

Talk about pregnancy discrimination.

Next up was child care. Would I have a place to put the baby while I was in class if I didn't graduate on time, as planned? I found out that although the university used to have day care on campus, the school's president had disbanded it a few years back to make way for more freshmen dorms (because we all know that packing those freshmen in like sardines equals big bucks for the college).

Housing was another disappointment. Once again, the university used to have family housing, but dissolved those dorms for the better-paying first-year students. Ben would still have an entire semester of classes and student teaching after my due date, so we would need to find a place to live.

And last on my list was financial aid. How would getting married and having a child affect my eligibility for financial aid? Would anything change?

Nobody knew. Everywhere I turned to for answers, I was met with blank stares and shoulder shrugs.

What I found out, through my official campus pregnancy investigation, was that my school offered a whole lot of nothing for a nontraditional student like myself. As it turns out, my school was not really unique.

Pregnant on Campus

A study done by Feminists for Life of America called *Perception Is Reality* surveyed college students across the United States and found that the majority of college and university campuses aren't equipped to handle the needs of pregnant and parenting students. Even schools that had adequate resources and support weren't making the cut, because students didn't know about the resources, or they weren't easily accessible and advertised; the perception that there was no help for pregnant and parenting students *became* the reality.

It doesn't help matters when you consider that, as the statistics show, the majority of women in college who become unexpectedly pregnant choose abortion or may drop out of school altogether, so the pressing need to establish more comprehensive services for pregnant and parenting students isn't really there. And the students who desperately need the resources and support aren't exactly loaded with tons of free time to organize a campaign on campus—they're slightly busy with raising kids, working multiple jobs, and going to school.

I admit that I took a personal affront to the whole situation. Pregnant and parenting students are an important part of campus life, and I hated that they might feel as though they didn't belong. In fact, most of the parents I met who were attending college were some of the most driven and motivated people I have ever met, so it would only make sense that the schools would want to help them succeed. So, why did people act like I was the first pregnant person to ever waddle through the college doors? It didn't make sense to me.

I set out to change things in a systematic approach, based on all the resources that I looked for and couldn't find for myself. I worked with the school and my student group on campus to create resources—including a parenting website, a student-parent support group, and awareness and educational programs, such as a student parent resources fair and training for financial aid.

Our efforts made a difference, not only to me personally, but to the campus as a whole. Near the end of the year, as students were clearing the campus, I found myself alone in the library, balancing to-do lists with my final exam notes. I sat quietly, rubbing my belly as the baby kicked and squirmed inside me. At first, the gentle fluttering against my abdomen had been easy to miss, but the baby had been growing stronger by the day. I thought about everything that I had managed to accomplish on campus that semester, and I realized that I was proud of myself.

While working as an advocate for pregnant and parenting students I found the strength to face my own pregnancy. The work I did my senior year was exhausting and at times overwhelming, but it was also a wonderful journey of self-discovery. I was able to realize my strength as a woman. I realized

> While working as an advocate for pregnant and parenting students I found the strength to face my own pregnancy.

that while the world may have seen me as just another pregnant, young girl, an unlucky statistic, or a person to be pitied, I had finally learned to walk my own path as a proud, pregnant college student. I realized that I had become stronger than I ever thought possible.

Young moms, student moms, pregnant students—we have had to hold our heads up high to disapproving looks, rude stares at our pregnant bellies and backpacks, and a society that wants women to choose either education and career or children. Our journeys may be difficult, but we can be reassured by the knowledge that we are truly showing the world that young moms have a place. And that place can be anywhere they choose.

So, why am I telling you all this? I want you to know that if you are a pregnant or parenting student wishing that things were different on your campus, realize that they can be! Honestly, the changes that I helped to implement were not difficult or time-consuming. And the thought that the school-sponsored website I helped to create is still up, helping other young moms and student parents? Infinitely rewarding.

You can make a difference for the pregnant and parenting students on your campus, too. To help you get started, I have included the very detailed guide "Thirteen Steps to Changing Your Campus" in the back of this book. Student-parent or not, you can help start the movement to change your own campus in support of pregnant and parenting students. Check out some of the resources I have on my website, or feel free to contact me if you need some help getting started.

CHAPTER TEN

What Else Do I Need to Know? What No One Tells You about Unplanned Pregnancy

Seven months pregnant with our second child and looking to furnish our newly purchased first home, my husband and I walked into a furniture store one blustery evening in March.

"Hi, can I help you?" asked the smoker-thin saleswoman with spiked blonde hair.

"Yes, we are interested in looking at some couches," I answered brightly, shifting our eighteen-month-old on my hip and adjusting my maternity shirt over my jeans.

The saleswoman paused.

"Well . . . ," she said, hesitantly glancing over her shoulder, apparently searching for backup or perhaps some less offensive customers.

She looked me up and down one more time, her eyes lingering on my belly and Ada's scuffed sneakers framing it.

"I can show you to our clearance section," she finally replied, gesturing vaguely toward the back of the store.

I knew my unplanned pregnancy would change a lot of things. But I didn't expect that the unplanned pregnancy would follow me even after I gave birth.

I wasn't prepared for all of the ways that my unplanned pregnancy would try to slowly intertwine its way into my life. I didn't realize how my guilt, shame, and the belief that I was irresponsible would threaten to pervade every aspect of my thinking. I've strug-

> I wasn't prepared for all of the ways that my unplanned pregnancy would try to slowly intertwine its way into my life.

gled with everything from fighting down waves of jealousy at "normal" baby showers and weddings to rude comments and questions if any of my children were "planned." I've fought against stereotypes for simply trying to go grocery shopping, hoping my clothes were nice enough or my children clean enough.

I've let my unplanned pregnancy threaten to rob me of my identity. It taunted me—telling me I would never be more than my bare ring finger or that I wouldn't succeed, that people would always look at me as "that girl who got pregnant."

My unplanned pregnancy was a death of sorts. After I had Ada, my life had shifted so dramatically from what I thought I would be doing after college graduation that I just couldn't find my footing. I felt like I was drifting. Drifting down a foggy river of night shifts, stretch marks, and a body I didn't recognize. I felt like I viewed everything through this lens of a surprise pregnancy—if I had messed up the motherhood part so badly, what good could I expect out of the rest of my life?

I was afraid of how to proceed as a young mom. What was I supposed to do? How I was supposed to act? I didn't know what the image of a good twenty-two-year-old mom looked like. Would she quit her job? Would she submit to her husband in all things? Would she scrapbook?

I had this vision of what being a mom meant—I wanted to be someone my kids could count on and look up to, but I struggled with finding my own path at the same time. I wondered how my children could look up to a mom for guidance on who they should be in life, if I was still figuring it out myself.

Working a job I hated to support us (I worked the night shift as a nurse on a cardiac floor at the time), feeling like I didn't even recognize myself anymore, and not knowing how to navigate my new life, *I think I just lost sight of who I was.*

And while I think a little bit of my problem was an actual clinical postpartum depression (I'll put on my OB nurse hat here for a minute and tell you, PPD is a real thing and you need to seek help if you experience similar symptoms, okay?), I started to see through my fog enough to realize that there was no "right" way to do motherhood. No one was judging me just because I

> I couldn't try to fit my life as a young mom into any type of prescribed path. It was time to create my own path.

had become a mother a bit earlier than I anticipated. I wasn't going to get a report card with a pass or failing grade.

I couldn't try to fit my life as a young mom into any type of prescribed path. It was time to create my own path.

So I tried to do just that. Strangely enough, I decided to go back to school. Going through the act of applying for and being accepted to graduate school jump-started my healing. It made me feel like I was still worthwhile. I wasn't just that girl who got pregnant. I still had brains, and I could still chase my dreams and make something of my life.

Former teen mom Gloria Malone also found that throwing herself into her schoolwork and routine helped to save her sanity. "I found that my 'happy place' was school," she told me. "It was the only consistent thing I had, so I held onto it for dear life." She encourages other moms to "find something that is a positive outlet or break from being a teen or young mom. It will make a huge difference!"

The three-hour drive to class once a week was actually refreshing to me; it was time to think and reflect; it provided silence for my soul. Getting lost in the swell of campus invigorated me and helped me to find my focus again. It felt good to be someone besides "Mom" for even a few short hours.

Although I haven't finished my graduate courses (I stopped classes right after my second daughter, Mya, was born two years and two days after her sister), I've realized the degree wasn't my real goal. *My real goal was finding myself again.* And although it's unfortunate that it cost me an additional student loan to do that, it has definitely been some of the best money I've ever spent. (I do, however, regret a few of the drive-through purchases made on the way home. Why is a McChicken sandwich so inviting at ten o'clock at night?)

Somewhere around Ada's first birthday, I felt like the fog was lifting. I started getting back into exercising. I grew out my hair (for some reason, I had gotten a "mom cut" during my pregnancy). I applied for a job on the day shift.

I started to forget trying to do what a mom was "supposed" to do and focused on what *I* wanted to do.

The struggle with unplanned pregnancy that no one mentions is the fact that so many mothers

> The struggle with unplanned pregnancy that no one mentions is the fact that so many mothers think that there is a "typical" way to do motherhood.

think that there is a "typical" way to do motherhood. For young moms, it can be easy to get disoriented and wonder what sort of path we are supposed to follow, because there aren't always a lot of great role models to choose from.

So, I've gathered up a few real-life role models of young moms who aren't afraid to share how they are following their own paths to motherhood. I admit that I have a secret (okay, so it's not so secret anymore) obsession with getting inside glimpses into the lives of other moms. It helps me to realize that I'm not crazy, that other moms struggle with finding the time to change out of their pajamas during the day, and many times, it inspires me to live a better life.

So, what does the real life of a young mom look like? Let's start with Raquel Kato, who we've already heard from a little bit in this book and who has almost the same exact story as me.

"There is no 'typical' day," Raquel says. "Every day is a new adventure, and that is the best thing about motherhood. However, at some point every day, there are at least two crying fits that can be somewhat stressful, there's usually some sort of leakage or poop explosion followed by an immediate bath, coffee is consumed, the baby naps, which is when I frantically try to get a million things done, but there is always a moment every day where I'm rocking my little girl to sleep and thinking to myself, *'this is the life.'*"

Raquel also finds maintaining her spiritual life helpful. "I go to daily Mass when I can and go to adoration once a week," she says. "Having that quiet time with God outside of daily prayers or devotions has been crucial for me. Whenever I slack on that relationship, I quickly feel myself becoming irritated and stressed. Making the effort to go to Mass or adoration is huge. Even if it's crazy hard to get there, if you put in the work, the Lord will reward you."

Jessica Watson knows the struggle of feeling "trapped" by young motherhood. "I think every young mother feels like she is struggling at one time or another," she said. "It is hard because, as a young mom, you are generally in the minority and the odds are stacked against you. My best advice is to remember that this time will pass. No matter how tough it is right now, this is just one more phase in your life. It will be behind you before you know it, and you will be wondering how you made it. The saying 'whatever doesn't kill you makes you stronger' is so true of being a young mom."

Mandy Lange says, "To me, being a mom means meeting your children as the loves of your life. I know I would sacrifice anything for Brady—my travel plans, my precious hours of sleep, my dream wedding, my vomit-free hair. And I would want to. I didn't really understand this kind of love until I met Brady officially, but I think being a mother isn't as much *what* you do as it is the fact that you *would* do anything, unconditionally, for your child. Including getting poop under your fingernails."

Kendra is a web designer (she designed my blog!) and a busy mom of two who just so happens to live in Hawaii. (I know, I know.) As a working mom, Kendra described how she keeps herself sane. "Talk to other moms. Be part of a play group or moms group. Call a friend on the phone," Kendra told me. "Make sure that you have conversations with other adults every day. Yes, talking to your baby is wonderful and magical and a blessing. But you also need grown-up conversation to stay sane!"

Getting together with other moms has been a lifesaver for me. Maybe once every few weeks, or even months, my set of "mom friends" and I will set up a play date of some sort. Nothing crazy, just an easy lunch or trip to the park to give us a chance to ignore our children and talk to each other. Sometimes, all we do is talk about our kids, but it doesn't matter. The point is to get that break and connect with other moms going through the same thing that you are.

Kendra also stresses the importance of taking time for yourself. "Even if it is painting your finger-nails and drinking a Diet Coke, just make sure that you do at least one thing for yourself each day," she says. "When I first had my little

> The point is to get that break and connect with other moms going through the same thing that you are.

girl, my husband [who would be gone at school almost the entire day] would come home and ask me, 'What did you do for yourself today?' So I always had to make sure I had something to report. I think that helped me settle into motherhood and realize that life wasn't over. I could still do fun things, pamper myself, take time to get ready in the morning, or go out. I wasn't 'trapped' in motherhood."

As for working or staying home? Kendra sums it up pretty nicely. "I think you have to do what you have to do," she says simply. "Some moms have to leave the home for work to provide income for the family. I do also think that there is a great reward in leaving the baby at home with a trusted babysitter and going to work one or two times a week. So either way, working or staying at home, just make sure you are in tune with what you and your baby need."

Former teen mom Emily is incredibly busy as a single mother and college student taking a "ridiculous nineteen credit hours," but she carves out meaningful (and affordable!) time with her son every week. "Tuesdays are our 'special dinners,'" said Emily. "We go to Denny's, because kids eat free. We both love this time to just sit, talk, and spend time together. Other days, we go to the library or bookstore, play at McDonald's, or just spend time at home playing *Just Dance 3*. Every single night I kiss him and say, 'I love you! I will miss you. You are my best friend!' before bed."

Bottom line? There is no right or wrong way to be a mom. Your life as an awesome young mom could mean starting your own business or working a few days a week, or a life full of play dates and cookies.

But I do want you to know that you have permission to decide just what "having it all" means to you—and the freedom to chase after your dreams.

> You have permission to decide just what "having it all" means to you—and the freedom to chase after your dreams.

And when I start to doubt that, drowning in a life of endless debt, diapers, and multiplying toys, I look at all the other amazing things that our fellow young mothers have done to live their dreams.

Here is a list of women who inspire me:

- Tara Pringle Jefferson took herself from laid off to a whole new career as a mommy blogger and writer in a mere seven months. She's a constant source of inspiration to me as a young mom, entrepreneur, writer, and author. Find her at theyoungmommylife.com.

- Jasmine Johnson took her unplanned pregnancy as a student at the University of Michigan and marched right on into medical school. She interviewed for medical school admission a mere eleven days after giving birth and is currently wrapping up her MD while pregnant with her second child. She blogs at mrsmommymd.com.

- Jacquelyn Kippenbrock went on to start her own successful photography business (J&J Bruise Photography).

- Emily of *Your Mom, the Blog* is pursuing her dream of getting her PhD while she courageously battles cancer.

- Darlene continued her love of traveling—just with baby in tow. She and her husband are saving up for a trip to Sweden and Norway with their current family of four. She blogs at youngmamatales.com.

- Kristin of *Little Mama Jama* overcame her struggle with postpartum depression and works from home as a writer and social media consultant.

- Shannon Oertle didn't let her unplanned pregnancy stop her from living her dream of becoming a writer and an artist. "Don't lose sight of your passions," says Shannon. "Just because you had kids young doesn't mean you can't still follow your dreams. You might just be taking a different route to them!"

- Jeanne Sanger of *Inside Out Motherhood* overcame bulimia and stereotypes about being a young mom when she became a successful writer. She has some really in-depth advice for young moms. You might want to grab a notebook. Seriously. Okay, are you ready? Here's Jeanne's advice: "Don't listen to the stereotypes. Just don't!"

- Katie of *Loyal, Loving, Learning* trusted that "God had a plan for us" when she learned that she and her boyfriend were expecting at the age of twenty-three. She is using her experiences as a young mom for inspiration to follow her dream of writing and illustrating a children's book.

- Young mom Hilary started up her own fitness company. She hightails it all around Massachusetts with her baby and stroller, whipping new moms into shape. If only she lived around my area . . .

- Taylor Shelton is proud of being a young mom, from misinterpreting her positive pregnancy test as a sophomore in college ("I saw the two lines and thought 'Phew!' remembers Taylor) to starting up her bakery business as a mom of two.

- Dwija of *House Unseen, Life Unscripted* is a fellow Catholic mom who didn't let having kids damper her wild and adventurous spirit. She and her husband bought a house—*off of the Internet without even looking at it first*—and moved their brood of six and counting across the country to live on the farm.

- Sarah of *The Mom Life* picked herself up from a pregnancy as a high school senior and a resulting abusive marriage to a career in banking. Young motherhood also has given Sarah the added bonus of being an early riser. "I actually like it!" laughs Sarah.

- Hannah Wingert, a young mom of three who is often mistaken for an older sister out in public with her brood, runs a successful online children's boutique.

- Jessica Watson is succeeding as a mom of four plus an angel, overcoming the death of one of her triplets, caring for her autistic daughter and as a blogger and breathtakingly beautiful writer. She writes at fourplusanangel.com

- Heidi Oran had her first pregnancy at age twenty-three and went on to found the Conscious Perspective, a movement to inspire social change through non-judgment, compassion, and tolerance.

- My dear cousin Mandy also became pregnant during her senior year of college and is now a wonderful mom to her man Brady, a wife to Ethan, a hilarious and heartfelt blogger, and in the process of finishing up her master's degree in education.

- Gloria Malone founded Teen Mom NYC and has made waves as a teen mother advocate, even appearing on the *O'Reilly Factor*. (Go Gloria!)

- Paula Rollo is a young mom taking great strides toward realizing her dream of becoming an author—all with her two young kids by her side.

- Miranda Gonzales and her husband welcomed a son early on in their young marriage, but Miranda still dreams of becoming a writer and started her own handmade accessories business.

- I love Lacy Stroessner's bravery to create the life she dreams of—she's a young mom, writer, and new farm owner! "This is the life I dreamed of," writes Lacy at her blog *Living on Love*.

- Perhaps one of my very favorite bloggers of all time, Michelle Horton is making waves with her movement, Early Mama. She writes for all kinds of prestigious places like *Babble* and *Parenting* on the ways that young motherhood is awesome.

- My writing idol Megan Francis, who became a mom at nineteen, went on to have five children, and build up a successful writing career from scratch says, "Don't feel like your life has to follow the 'normal' linear path for you to be successful. You don't have to go straight from high school to college, finish in four years, and immediately move on to the career world. Take some time off if you want. Take this opportunity to redefine what success would look like to you. Take chances. Believe in yourself as a mom and as a capable adult. You can still follow any dream you put your mind to!"

As all of these inspiring young moms show, it doesn't take a responsible age or the right career or the perfect degree to make you a good mom. Don't let your unplanned pregnancy or your status as a young mom make you feel like you have something to prove, because you don't. You already *are* a good mom. You are working or going to school and making it happen. You are chasing your dreams and serving as a good example for your kids.

You *can* carve your own path to motherhood, and God does want to support you on your journey.

You *can* do this.

You *are* a good mother.

And you are not alone.

If you are sufficiently pumped up now and I have been successful in my mission in writing this book, I suggest that we get on with the business of taking over the world, one young mom at a time . . .

Right after I change this dirty diaper.

Additional Resources

Early Mama's Questions to Consider Before Marriage

~~~~~~

I will reiterate the sentiment that it is extremely important to sit down with a spiritual advisor to discuss the vocation of marriage, but you may also find these extremely practical questions to consider before marriage by Michelle Horton of *Early Mama* helpful.

1. What's your credit/debt situation?

This is one of those situations where you have to try and step outside of the lovey-dovey romance and assess all of the things you don't like to think about. There might be clues—blatant, obvious clues—that you're choosing not to see.

First of all, is your partner in a massive amount of debt? I'm not talking about school loans (we all have school loans), but did he/she accumulate a heaping mound of credit card and loan debt? Are there creditors constantly calling and sending threatening letters? No one goes into a marriage assuming the worst, but if the worst does end up happening—if he leaves you and decides to default on all of his debt—then *you* will be held responsible.

Also: what's his/her credit score? You might think it's ridiculous and insulting to consider something as trivial as a *credit score* before saying "I do," but it's actually a telling insight into your financial future. Not only that, but if you're going to be applying for big, important loans together (like, say, a house), they look at *both* of your credit scores. So that measly number can end up costing you more in interest—or even cost you a house—which is money out of your pocket and stress added to your life.

Don't overlook big financial blunders—as tempting as it is to give the benefit of the doubt. Is he defaulting on child support payments? Is he drowning in unrealistic car payments? Gambling debt? Borrowing too much from friends and family? These types of situations aren't just about money—they're about character, judgment, and maturity.

This isn't to say that you should leave this financial disaster. But maybe the goal of marriage could motivate you guys to clear up the credit blemishes and make smarter financial decisions, without the added financial and legal risks of marriage. And when financial issues are such a major stress on marriage—especially younger, financially inexperienced couples—it might be a good idea to get a handle on money issues before entering a marriage.

2. Do you need benefits?

Insurance is a big deal. And navigating the tricky world of health insurance while you're pregnant is an even bigger deal. If choosing marriage also means the loss of insurance protection under your parents' plan, as it did for me, you will have to research other available insurance plans. Ensuring that you and your baby's health are taken care of is a top consideration and in some cases, may be cause enough to delay a wedding.

3. Are you/Can you be financially independent?

Young marriages can be challenging enough—the most important thing you can do is to protect yourself and your family. Having at least the *option* for financial security is, ultimately, a smart move.

And the hard truth is that in today's economically challenged times, you never know what will happen. My husband was still in school for a full year after we were married, and then he was laid off twice in his first year of employment as a teacher. I can't tell you how important it was to me and our marriage to know that I could support our family full time. We were partners in this, and I do think it is important for a woman to have the know-how and security to have the peace of mind that comes from knowing she could care for her family if need be.

4. Are you going through a big change right now?

Pregnancy is, quite possibly, the biggest change you'll ever go through. Especially if this was an unexpected pregnancy at an unexpectedly young age. You have hormonal surges, lifestyle changes—sometimes anxiety, depression, general freaking out. In all honesty, this might not be the best time to make another life-changing decision. Assess your emotional state before saying "I do." You can always get married later—but it's much more difficult to undo that decision.

5. Is there something you want to change about this person?

Are you hoping that he'll eventually stop smoking two joints a day? Or that he'll outgrow his video game obsession? Or that he'll get some ambition in his life? At the same time, is there something about *you* that your partner is trying to change?

You cannot—cannot—go into a marriage expecting something about that person to eventually change, because it very well might not. You can either accept that person wholeheartedly, or perhaps put a halt on the marriage discussion.

This is also an important time to assess how the two of you communicate, and if you have any major trust issues. So many marriage experts say that it's important to be your own person before you can belong to someone else. That you have to grow up before you can grow together. And if one or both of you has a lot of maturing left to do, why stack the odds against you? Of course you'll continue to grow in a marriage, but it's a smart question to ask yourself while weighing the pros and cons.

6. Why are you getting married?

Be honest with yourself and 'fess up about the real reasons that you're getting married. Is it to please your family? To do "the right thing?" To have a storybook wedding?

Know your reasons for getting married, because in the end, they're all that matters. And as Meaghan Francis, author, writer, and young mom turned mother of five, says,

> Don't make permanent decisions based on temporary problems. When you're facing an early, unexpected pregnancy, everything can feel like a crisis. You might be tempted to completely uproot your life or make huge, sweeping changes to accommodate your new reality, but the fact is, pregnancy doesn't last forever, and neither does new motherhood. In a year or two, whether you marry your partner or don't, whether you move away or stay where you are, whether you stay in school or drop out, your life will have calmed down and become your "new normal," and you'll be in a much better position to decide on your next steps.

In applying her perfect advice to the marriage question, remember—you're not marrying your priest or your parents—you're marrying the man you will live with for the rest of your life. Ultimately, your marriage is just between the two of you.

Thirteen Steps to Changing Your Campus

My quick-and-dirty guide to changing your campus in support of pregnancy and parenting resources.

1. Assess the campus.

You can't know what your school offers for pregnant and parenting students if you don't look! Oftentimes, students are surprised by what their school actually has. Feminists for Life offers the best tool I have found for assessing the complete scope of pregnant and parenting resources on campus with their Pregnancy Resources Survey. You can take it online at www.surveymonkey.com/s/FFLU and print your results. The survey can help you personally as a pregnant or parenting student, and it can help you identify the resources that need some work on your campus.

2. Investigate the health center.

One of the first places that a pregnant student might turn to is to the campus health center. When I took my pregnancy test at the campus health center, it was a mortifying experience because the clinic was set up in an open-floor layout that required checking in at the front desk—so everyone in the place could hear what you were there for.

The day I went, it happened that a male classmate was running the desk, and he couldn't hear me when I mumbled what I was there for.

"What's that you say?" he boomed. "You're here for a pregnancy test?"

Mortified, I nodded and slinked into the corner as inconspicuously as I could.

As you know, my visit to the health center that day didn't really go all that smoothly. The nurse practitioner who administered my pregnancy test informed me that I was indeed pregnant and then proceeded to ask me how I would tell my parents. I had been able to keep my composure up until then, when I of course burst into tears. As I struggled to keep it together, I asked her a few questions about my options and what help I could find on campus. Was there insurance I could buy? Was there anyone I could talk to?

Unfortunately, the nurse had no answers and walked out on me, leaving me alone and crying in her office. It wasn't a great start to my pregnancy, and frankly, it wasn't a great move professionally on her part. It wasn't until a few weeks later, when I had settled down and regained the ability to think about my pregnancy without bawling that I realized just how frightening the treatment I had received at the center was. I was in a pretty good position to have an unplanned pregnancy—I had a fiancé, a supportive family, a job, a place to live, and was really close to graduation—and yet, my pregnancy still threw me completely for a loop. I still had so many questions, and I felt completely lost. I tried to imagine how it would have felt had I turned up in her office that day like a lot of other women in my position—alone, without a boyfriend or even supportive family, maybe not even a place to live or a job—and had been treated that way.

I hated the thought that a woman in that position would have received no help or support. I decided to schedule a follow-up meeting with the director of the health center to address the issue of how our school could respond better to pregnant women.

When I walked into the meeting a few days later, I discovered, much to my dismay, that the director of health services was actually the same nurse who administered my pregnancy test.

The director remembered me and told me how busy she was that day and that she was rushed because I was a walk-in. She told me that I should have made an appointment, rather than just drop in.

My apologies for not scheduling my unplanned pregnancy.

In all seriousness, I remember pacing the hallways of school for an hour before I worked up the nerve to go into health services that day. It was hard enough to walk in, let alone actually call and schedule an appointment. I probably never would have showed up. It's a huge step to reach out for help. (Yes, I'm talking to you!)

The director eventually broke down and told me that she had felt bad about what happened, but she just wasn't aware of the resources and support on campus or in the community that could have helped me.

If the director of health services on campus wasn't aware of any resources to help a pregnant student, then who would be?

At the end of the meeting, the director was in complete agreement that something needed to change and that the school should offer additional resources for other women like me. I was thrilled that she was so open to working together and surprised that I had made a difference. We scheduled a follow-up meeting with her boss to continue up the chain of command, working for resources and support for pregnant and parenting students.

At our next meeting, imagine my surprise when I found that the clinic had been completely revamped and organized! She had taken my suggestions to heart and rearranged the clinic to offer full privacy for students and updated their check-in process. Success!

Your mission, should you choose to accept it, is to set up a meeting with the director of your on-campus or local community health center to walk through the process of how a pregnant woman is treated.

3. Provide health resources.

In conjunction with researching your school's health center, you will want to be sure that pregnant students are receiving accurate information about health resources at the center and in the local community. For instance, pregnant students need to be provided with information about how to obtain Medicaid and sign up for the Women, Infants, and Children program (WIC).

- *WIC.* We touched on WIC earlier, and although I didn't have the greatest experience with it, I know plenty of women who have benefited from the program. Some states make it easy to use and load all your benefits on a credit card so you can swipe and go. Women can apply for WIC at your local health department. Find your state health department here: www.cdc.gov/mmwr/ international/relres.html

- *Insurance.* Many school insurance plans don't cover pregnancy, so pregnant students will want to get started on health insurance, as soon as possible. Not only will prenatal visits start almost immediately, but there's always the risk of not getting coverage because pregnancy can be considered a "pre-existing" condition. If women are not eligible to purchase any type of private or personal insurance, check out the federal insurance of Medicaid. Remind them not to be embarrassed or ashamed to use Medicaid. It will save so much money in the long run, and remember, it's an investment! A mother and her and child should both be eligible for Medicaid if she is a pregnant or parenting student. Medicaid can also be used as a secondary insurance—that way, if the primary insurance doesn't cover all of the costs associated with the pregnancy, Medicaid can pick up the rest. Medicaid also covers a pregnant woman for the duration of her pregnancy and up to six weeks postpartum (this is where Medicaid saved my life!) and should cover the baby for at least one year after he or she is born, without having to reapply for coverage. Women can apply for Medicaid by going to the local Health & Human Services office. Each state has its own health department rules, so visit this website: www.cdc.gov/mmwr/international/relres. html to find your state's information. You can also visit the official Medicaid website here: www.medicaid.gov/ index.html. Find out about insuring children through a federal insurance program here: www.insurekidsnow. gov/state/index.html

4. Find a student-parent support group.

And if one doesn't exist, start one. Seriously, it's not that hard, and the support you will receive can be invaluable. The hardest part of going through college as a pregnant student was just feeling so alone. I felt like a freak of nature, both in size and situation, waddling around campus. The student-parent support group that I started helped me in meeting other moms and hearing their stories. The women out there who are making it all work are *amazing*. Set up a Facebook page, post flyers, host a contest or event on campus, or run your own resources fair to connect. Together with some awesome friends, we started a student-parent support group, called SUPPORT, which stood for Supporting Unplanned Pregnancies, Parents, and Organizing Resources Together. Clever, no? I'm obviously still proud of that title, as I had to write a whole book just to tell you about it.

Our group coordinated efforts for all of the resource-based initiatives on campus that year, but more importantly, at least to me, we had meetings and invited all the pregnant and parenting students on campus to just sit and talk (okay, and eat cookies . . . can you have a meeting of pregnant women without food?) about our experiences. I cried during a lot of those meetings, but they saved my life. I met incredible women whom I still follow on Facebook, because I'm just in awe of how they have succeeded as young mothers.

As a group, we also hosted the country's first-ever Rally for Resources with Feminists for Life (more on that later) and sponsored a student-parent essay contest, where we were able to petition the school administration for more resources and provide some financial assistance to three student parents through donations. Having a student-parent support group not only showed our school that student parents mattered; it brought us together and kept us all going strong when we felt like giving up.

5. Provide counseling.

Our group worked to put together a resources brochure and packet for the health center to distribute to any women who came in for pregnancy testing and coordinated care with the counseling office so that any woman with a positive test could receive an automatic referral to see a counselor. Sometimes, it just helps to have someone to talk to.

The counseling office was in urgent need of some crisis pregnancy training. When I met with some of the staff and student volunteers in the counseling office, they were pretty defensive at first. They were professionals already, right? They knew how to handle anything that came their way.

So I asked one student counselor—a young girl with long, blonde hair that fell neatly down her back—what she would say to a young woman who had just received a positive pregnancy test.

She blinked at me for a minute and then splayed out a handful of brochures on the table in front of me with a flourish. "I would go over these," she said triumphantly.

People, they were *birth control* brochures.

I'm not making this stuff up. Is *this* how our colleges are equipped to handle the needs of pregnant students? Tell me again how a brochure on birth control is going to help a pregnant woman. Needless to say, I had to have a little chat with that counselor's boss (I was nice, I promise), and he initiated an office-wide training and intervention program specifically tailored for pregnant students. No more handing out birth control brochures as a way to "help" pregnant students. I may be going out on a limb here, but I'm pretty sure that ship has sailed when those two lines show up.

If counseling is a separate office from the health center at your school, be sure to set up a meeting with the counseling director to talk about all of the ways a pregnant woman and her partner can feel supported.

6. Make sure financial aid knows the rules about pregnant women.

When I found out I was pregnant, my thoughts naturally turned toward my finances. Or more specifically, to my lack thereof. I decided to pay a little visit to the financial aid office to see if there was any additional assistance available for pregnant or parenting students that might help me make it to graduation without collapsing in a giant exhausted and pregnant puddle.

And found nada.

So, I did what a lot of girls do and vented to my dad. *Who* just so happens to work for a college. *Who* just so happened to look into some financial aid policies. *Who* just so happened to find out that a pregnant student can claim her unborn child as a dependent on her FAFSA.

Yeah, I know.

Back to the financial aid office I marched with that little nugget of information. I set up a meeting with a counselor to discuss how I could claim my baby and, thus, qualify for some additional financial aid.

He told me, essentially, that I was crazy.

I demanded that he check with his boss.

He repeated the sentiment that I was, indeed, crazy.

I repeated the demand that he check with his supervisor.

Ten minutes later, he returned, policy in hand, and I filed my paperwork that granted me an additional two thousand dollars in grant money.

I was so excited that I immediately sent two members of my student-parent group, both pregnant, into the financial aid office so that they could apply for more assistance, too. They met with the *same* officer that I had, and can you guess what he told them?

Yup.

That they were crazy.

Clearly, college financial aid officers aren't used to pregnant women. Perhaps I'm overreacting, but I felt like these men expected us pregnant women to take care of our "problem" or drop out instead of pestering them with demands for more financial aid. Ugh.

Needless to say, however, I didn't go away. I set up another meeting with the director of financial aid this time, printed out the policy and highlighted it, and got him to agree to a training for his staff so that they would be familiar with the policies pertaining to pregnant mothers.

So what is the policy?

Straight from the FAFSA website:

An unborn child who will be born during the 2013–2014 award year may also be counted in the household size if the parents, or independent student and spouse, will provide more than half of the child's support through the end of the 2013–2014 award year (June 30, 2014).

Women who are pregnant at the time they fill out the FAFSA can include an unborn child on the "household size" section. If she becomes pregnant during the school year and the baby is due before the end of the year, she can update her dependency status and change the status to "independent student." Note that the policy states that the mother will need to provide half of the financial support for the baby, so if she is planning on adopting or having her family support the baby, she may not be eligible.

I was able to fill out the paperwork to add my unborn baby as a dependent and received the Pell grant—almost two thousand dollars that didn't need to be repaid—as a result.

You can find the whole document here: http://studentaid.ed.gov/es/sites/default/files/2013-14-completing-fafsa.pdf. The policy is on page fifteen.

So, repeat after me: pregnant women can count their unborn babies on the FAFSA! And don't let any financial aid officer tell you otherwise. *Hmmphh*. Find the official policy on the FAFSA website here: http://studentaid.ed.gov/es/sites/default/files/2013-14-completing-fafsa.pdf

7. Connect student parents to baby gear.

The thing about baby gear is that no one uses it for very long. Remember, babies grow quickly. So you can find a lot of used baby stuff in great condition. I've bought a lot of my baby and kid gear secondhand or used hand-me-downs. Mom-to-mom sales are my lifesavers; I even bought my breast pump used, which might sound kind of gross, but those things are so expensive! And I swear I sanitized it thoroughly. Baby swaps are also popping up everywhere. In fact, I just joined one on Facebook, and it seems like a genius idea. A lot of my baby gear is still in good shape, even after three kids, so it makes sense that I could swap with other moms in different stages than me. Another reliable option for women in need of baby gear is to look for a local pregnancy resource center. Clients might need to go through their program, but they can usually provide all of the gear a mother will need. You can find a local pregnancy care center near you by doing a search or using the pro-life OptionLine service (www.optionline.org). OptionLine also has a nice feature that you can use to chat online with someone. Sometimes, a woman just needs someone to talk to.

8. Host a pregnant and parenting resources fair.

As I rounded the corner on my third trimester, I knew I wanted to do something big on campus—go out with a bang, so to speak, other than the one left every time I ran into something with my giant belly. So I worked with Feminists for Life on planning a resource fair for pregnant and parenting students—the nation's first ever Rally for Resources.

When our club began planning our resource fair, I was struck by the desperate need to change the social stigmas attached to being a student parent. I have worked so hard to find the resources that are available to students like me, only to find that using those resources is often associated with shame.

To host our fair, I contacted every resource, both on campus and in the community, that I could think of to join us by hosting a table or providing their resources or materials for us to hand out to students. A sample of some of the organizations I invited included:

- Local Red Cross chapter
- WIC office
- Financial aid office (on campus)
- Counseling services (on campus)
- Health services (on campus)
- Babies "R" Us
- Local photographers
- President of the university
- School newspaper
- Medicaid Office
- Head Start
- Local child care centers
- Local doctor's offices
- Medicaid office representative
- Parenting coalitions
- Pregnancy centers
- Local pro-life organizations

For a fun twist for the event, I also invited a local massage and beauty school, whose students were able to provide free hairstyles, manicures, and massages for credit while we enjoyed a little pampering! I asked for some donations of money, too, and was able to purchase food for the event (*hellooo*, this was a fair for pregnant women) and provide a cash prize to the winners of the student-parent essay contest we sponsored.

A few weeks before the fair, I posted flyers all over campus advertising a student-parent essay contest. The contest's purposes were twofold: not only was I able to actually find the student parents who were hiding on campus, but I was able to hear their stories and present them to the school administration. As I mentioned earlier, the struggle with student parents is that they are so incredibly good at their jobs—you know, raising kids, working, and going to school— that they don't have a lot of visibility on campus. The school administration doesn't really cater to them, because they don't have to.

I hoped to change that. And the essays I received were real stories from real student parents that I was able to take the school's president and say, "See? These students do exist, and they do have needs!"

The event was a big success. Some of the awesome members of my group also ran a T-shirt making booth, where we did iron-on decals and baby "footprints," that was a big hit. We also ran a continual petition that students could sign in support of more resources on campus, which we also turned in to the university's president.

9. Check out child care.

So what was the number one need that we heard from student parents on campus?

Child care.

Hands down, no comparison.

And what was the only thing that our school didn't offer in any capacity?

Child care.

It is my great sadness in life that we were not able to change the child-care situation on my campus. At my school, like a lot of schools, the biggest issue was funding a child-care center. Apparently, kids are expensive. Who knew?

A lot of schools offer on-site day care, but there are a lot of problems with them:

1. They are ridiculously expensive. Like, more than a home mortgage.

2. They accept faculty's children first, leaving little room for poor students.

3. They don't accept babies. So unless you plan on giving birth to a toddler, you may be out of luck.

Federal programs exist to help student parents afford child care (and don't forget, all that child care is a tax write-off!) or help you urge your school to apply for a grant to start a child care program on campus. You can find more information on that here: www2.ed.gov/programs/campisp/index.html.

If your school can apply for a grant, the administration may be able to start a child-care program on campus. One way many schools are able to finance a child-care center is by utilizing students in early education programs to staff the center as part of their schooling. It's a win-win!

Check with the financial aid office on your campus first to see if there are any programs available to help students find child care. Start by checking with the Office of Child Care through the US Department of Health and Human Services for more information on finding help to pay for child care: www.acf.hhs.gov/programs/occ/parents.

The National Coalition for Campus Children's Centers also runs an online list of campus child-care centers and child-care resources, so you can check if your state or school has one: http://campuschildren.org/links.html. You can also add your school to the list if it's missing!

And I would also like to take this time to point out that aside from the obvious times that you are in class, student parents might find it helpful to schedule some study time when they have a babysitter booked. I also found Child Care Aware (www.childcareaware.org) through the Higher Education Alliance of Advocates for Students with Children (www.heaasc.org). That site is nice because you can just plug in your zip code to bring up child care near you.

10. Help with housing.

If your school doesn't offer family housing, as many don't, you know that student parents will need to make some decisions about where the best place is to live with their children. I suggest that you first start by setting up a meeting with your school's president or housing officer to ask if a few dorms could be set aside for family housing; that way you aren't asking for the creation of any new dorms or any special treatment—you are just asking for the same right that every other student has.

The US Department of Housing and Urban Development has resources to help students find subsidized housing or renter's assistance: http://portal.hud.gov/hudportal/HUD?src=/topics/rental_assistance. Resources like Temporary Assistance for Needy Families may help parents pay for housing if they are in an especially difficult financial crisis: www.hhs.gov/children/index.html.

11. Provide breast-feeding support.

For mothers who are breast-feeding, or for those who plan to breast-feed, try reaching out to the women's resource center on campus for help and support. They may be able to help you figure out a lactation space where you can pump during the day. Breast-feeding, even while in school, may help you stay connected to your baby when you're away and focused (or stressed) about school. By law, your school or workplace does need to provide you a private place (that isn't a bathroom!) for women to pump or feed their babies, so don't let anyone make you feel like breast-feeding support is not important.

12. Consider everything else.

And then there are the miscellaneous things you can help pregnant and parenting students with, such as:

- *Jobs.* Check into work-study options that will help off-set the cost of student loans, or better yet, help student parents to apply for work at a day care! Babysitting and making money? Win-win!

- *Time Management.* Pretty sure this could be an entire book in itself, but after years in the trenches, I will only offer two pieces of advice for student parents:

  1. Save the tasks that require the most concentration for when the baby is asleep. Do not, I repeat, do not, fall into the trap of "just cleaning up real quick" after you the lay the baby down. I have done this more times than I can count, and I can guarantee you that the second you sit down to work after tidying up for "just a second," the baby will wake up. Resist the urge to do anything but work on homework or tasks that require your utmost concentration when

the baby is sleeping or with a babysitter. Save the other mindless tasks (laundry, dishes, etc.) for when the baby is awake.

2. Always make a plan. Whether you use a fancy app or plain old notebook paper, always make a daily, weekly, and monthly plan. If you don't have a to-do list or goal sheet that you can easily access, you will find that in the moments that you miraculously have a free minute, you will be so flustered or exhausted that you won't even know where to start. So, keep a list handy, and with one glance, you will have a game plan for action.

- *Stress.* I wish I had some kind of magic advice here. But honestly, all of those columns and articles that encourage moms to "take time for themselves" always just serve to make me more stressed out. Working, writing a research paper, being up with the baby, looking longingly at my pants that used to fit—and I'm supposed to add "me time" into all of that? Sometimes, it just feels like another thing I need to feel guilty about for not doing. So while I will encourage you to take a breather every now and then, even if it's for an hour to grab a coffee by yourself, I wouldn't stress too much about "me time." Instead, I would encourage you to keep your eye on the prize and know that this time in your life is temporary. And yeah, yeah, I know you have to treasure each and every moment because "they grow so fast," but have faith in yourself. There is no shame for recognizing that this time in your life is hard and that it's an investment in a brighter future. Also in related news . . .

- *Chocolate.* Oops, how did that get in there?

- *Scholarships.* Do a quick Google search or check your school's financial aid office for local, private scholarships. Sometimes they are in small amounts, but they can really add up. I would also check with your local pregnancy center and pro-life coalition. Many times, they are very supportive of pregnant students. The HEAASC also has a list of some scholarships for students: www.heaasc.org/Default.aspx?pageId=1225167

13. Create a pregnant and parenting resources website.

After you've done all of these things listed in the guide you can take everything that you've learned and compile it all on a website so you can share your knowledge with other students. Perhaps my crowning jewel of achievement on campus was the creation of a comprehensive pregnant and parenting resources website for my school. I worked with the director of Health and Counseling Services to create a one-stop shop for all things pregnant and parent related on our campus.

The site I created still stands today: www.svsu.edu/phe/health education/sexualhealth/pregnancyservicesresources and it makes me so proud to think that the work we did could be helping other pregnant women and student parents on campus.

Establishing a website that lists all the resources on campus and in the community is vitally important for colleges. It's literally the first thing a pregnant woman will want to access, and it shows that a college cares about all of its students, not just the traditional party-hopping coeds.

If your school doesn't have a website, I recommend that you use the sample forms and guides by Feminists for Life to get started: www.feministsforlife.com/cop/index.htm. They cover everything that you should include on your website, from paternity-services support to child care to pregnant athletes on a scholarship.

List of Resources for Pregnant and Parenting Students

- CDC State Health Departments: www.cdc.gov/mmwr/international/relres.html

- US Department of Housing and Urban Development: http://portal.hud.gov/hudportal/HUD?src=/topics/rental_assistance

- Feminists For Life Pregnancy Resources: www.feministsfor-life.com/resources/index.htm

- Free Application for Federal Student Aid: www.fafsa.ed.gov/

- Heartbeat International (a crisis pregnancy center provider): www.heartbeatinternational.org.

- Higher Education Alliance: www.heaasc.org/Default.aspx?pageId=1225167

- Medicaid/Child Insurance: www.medicaid.gov/index.html. Find out about insuring your child through a federal insurance program here: www.insurekidsnow.gov/state/index.html.

- National Campus Resource Directory for Pregnant and Parenting Students: www.feministsforlife.com/campusresources/index.php

- OptionLine: www.optionline.org

- Students for Life of America: http://pregnantoncampus.studentsforlife.org

- Temporary Cash Assistance: www.nccp.org/profiles/index_36.html

Favorite Young-Mom Blogs

Just a few of my favorite young-mom blog haunts. These are all moms that inspire me, make me laugh, and remind me that I'm not alone in this young-mom journey. Of course I have a full list on my own blog: www.tinybluelines.com.

- *The Amateur Mom*: thoughtsofanamateur.wordpress.com
- *Early Mama*: www.earlymama.com
- *Embrace Grace*: www.embracegrace.com
- *The Happiest Home*: www.happiesthome.com
- *The Story of A Rose*: raquelrkato.wordpress.com
- *The Young Mommy Life*: www.theyoungmommylife.com

Talking Guide for Religious and Pro-life Organizations

When I found out I was pregnant, my first thought was to seek help. I was terrified and in denial, and I turned to the first place that I thought of—my university's health center.

When I finally worked up the courage to walk in, I took yet another pregnancy test and waited for the result. When the nurse practitioner called me into her office, there was no denying it any longer—I was pregnant.

As I broke down in uncontrollable tears in her office and asked basic questions, like how I would get health insurance or where could I find prenatal care, the nurse simply shrugged her shoulders.

My sobs filled the room as she examined her chart in silence. After a few minutes, she stood up and said, "I have other patients to see, but you can stay in here if you want." She closed the door behind her, walking out on me without so much as an offer of a Kleenex.

Your first words to a woman facing an unplanned pregnancy matter.

I know that many people have good intentions of helping young women like me who face unplanned pregnancy; but the truth is, it's very easy to say the wrong thing. Your words, however well intentioned they may be, just might alienate her and turn her away.

I know how sensitive I was during my pregnancy. I resented that people assumed I was in need of spiritual guidance or looking for a handout. The simple fact of the matter was that I was a normal, Christian young woman who had made a mistake. We all make mistakes, and we all sin. I was not so different from any of you—my life was not forever doomed, nor did I require teams of spiritual leaders to lift me up in prayer.

What I *did* need was help in accepting my pregnancy and believing that it could be a good thing. What I *didn't* need was people reminding me that I had sinned, or reminding me to "think of the baby," or long, rambling lectures on the preciousness of life.

I urge you to take it from me—a former president and founder of my college's first pro-life club, a strong Christian, a registered nurse, a professional speaker and advocate for women, and most important, a mother and wife—and educate yourself on some ways that you can find the *right* words to best help a woman who may be facing an unplanned pregnancy. It is so important for us to realize that often, the very Christian values we hold dear can drive a woman to feel she has no other choice but to turn to abortion. Shame, guilt, and fear of judgment from other Christians are powerful motivators to a woman reeling from the shock of an unplanned pregnancy. Even after I had chosen life for my baby, it was a constant struggle against the condemnation of Christian pro-life leaders I encountered. We must realize that our actions—and our words—to women facing crisis pregnancies can turn the tide against abortion.

1. **Realize that she is in a crisis.** It's called a "crisis" pregnancy for a reason. Women facing unplanned pregnancy enter a very real and normal state of shock. The initial news about a pregnancy will leave a woman reeling, panicked, and unable to think clearly. A further complication of the shock state is that a woman simultaneously enters a period of grief and actual mourning for her "lost" life, which can come and go in circular patterns. You should know that women in these early, and sometimes even later, stages of crisis think

irrationally and are prone to self-preservation. Logical, clear reasoning will get you nowhere with her at this stage. What you need to do is focus on showing complete support for her. Some tips:

- *Avoid reacting.* Think "poker face" here. You will never be able to predict all the situations that women face. The worst thing you can do is to show any type of shocked reaction—it will make her feel that her already desperate situation is even more shocking.

- *Encourage her to make her own decision.* Don't offer up any advice in the early stages. Trust her mother's intuition and encourage her to explore her wishes about the pregnancy. Support her to be honest about what she— and no one else—wants.

- *When in doubt, remember these words: "It's okay."* In the beginning stages, this is all I wanted to hear. I just wanted reassurance—real or not—that everything would be okay. Of course, there was no guarantee that things would be okay, and I knew that, but it still didn't change the fact that I wanted to hear the words.

- *Don't convey disappointment.* She is already inflicting enough self-punishment on herself. The guilt and shame associated with an unplanned pregnancy can be overwhelming; usually, she is already disappointed in herself for the actions that have led her there. Don't fuel the fire.

  Example: "It really is going to be okay, Megan, and I promise it will get better. You are a strong woman, and you have a lot of people supporting you. Know that we are here for whatever you need."

2. **Tread the religious ground carefully.** Navigating the religious aspect of an unplanned pregnancy can be tricky; on one hand, you know that prayer and a relationship with God will help her in the end, but I can't stress enough how important it is to let her come to her own understanding of her spirituality. As I mentioned earlier, I struggled with guilt and "hid" from God for the first half of my pregnancy. During that time, I resented any religious talk or attempts to "save" me. I needed time to find my way back to God on my own. Many women have shared with me that they have struggled with guilt and avoided religious activities in the beginning, so be careful not to push anything on her until she is ready, or you may lose her altogether. Other considerations for treading the religious tightrope:

- *Don't assume she is in a religious crisis.* You may alienate her, especially if she is already feeling conflicted about her religious beliefs in contrast to what she has done. Jumping into prayer or spouting off biblical verses may just send her over the edge.

- *It is okay to congratulate her.* The message surrounding her is that this pregnancy is a bad thing. If not an outright mistake, then at the very least bad timing. People pity her, look down on her, or walk on eggshells around her. Don't make a parade out of it, but don't be afraid to offer up a simple "congrats," either. She needs to hear—and believe—that this baby *is* a good thing. But be careful not to go overboard on talking about the baby. Too much, and she might be scared away, so keep it short and simple.

Example: "I heard your news, Sarah, and I just wanted to say congratulations. I hope your first trimester goes easily for you!"

3. **Focus on her.** In the beginning, the last thing she is thinking about is the fact that there is a real, living baby inside of her. It just feels so unreal. She needs time to come to terms with the life that she has now lost—her own—before she can focus on the baby, and that's okay. I promise you, she *will* come around, but right now, the last thing she can think about is the baby. She will come to the place and time over the next nine months when she is ready to focus on the baby, but right now, she needs to focus on herself and so do you. Not to mention, it's a lifelong lesson she will need to learn. She will always need to place the oxygen mask on herself first. Focus your energy into supporting the mom and what she needs right now. That means putting the baby booties away for now. Instead, try a few of the suggestions below.

- *Be real.* Share a story about your own pregnancy, make a joke about morning sickness, or relate an experience you've seen another young mom go through. Don't be afraid to let your guard down a little—you may be a "professional" or someone she is relying on for guidance, but showing your human side will help her relate to you even more.

- *Don't try to solve all of her problems at once.* There's usually more to the picture than just a pregnancy—college scholarships, relationships, parents, jobs. Don't get lost in the big picture just yet. Take it one day at a time. Today, just offer support.

- *Don't assume that she needs help.* This was one of my biggest pet peeves. Even after I became a professional speaker and advocate for young moms, people would still come up to me after my talks and offer me cribs and changing tables. Um, what? Just because a young woman is in a crisis pregnancy doesn't mean every part of her life is in a crisis. We aren't all looking for handouts. It's a natural reaction to want to offer help, so if you feel strongly about it, please, just simply ask her what she needs.

- *Suggest that she take time for herself.* This is the perfect opportunity to suggest that she take a "day off." Surprise her with a gift certificate to get her nails done, or suggest she pay a visit to your massage therapist. Treat to her to coffee or a lunch out. Show her that you really do care about her first.

    Example: "Lydia, I know it seems like everyone is pressuring you right now. I want you to take a day off and just focus on yourself. I know how much you love to read, so I got you this gift certificate to the local bookstore. I hope you can spend an afternoon there to just relax. You deserve it!"

4. **Encourage her.** There is so much emphasis on all the hard parts about being a young mom. From the TV shows about young mothers to the campaigns against teenage pregnancy, the message is always the same: pregnancy is a plague to be avoided. Even as a married woman, my sister-in-law, who became a mom at age twenty-one, was bombarded by negative messages from family and friends about how hard it

would be to juggle being young and having a baby. Trust me, pregnant young women are well aware that it's going to be hard, and one of the toughest blocks you will have to break through to help her to choose life is breaking through that negative thinking. Her thinking, *I don't think I can do this,* will quickly become, *I can't do this,* and a trip to the abortion clinic if all she ever hears are negative comments about the hardships of young motherhood. Help her by encouraging her from the get-go. You need to believe that she can succeed, and your confidence in her will catch on. Try these encouraging motivators:

- *Don't judge.* It should go without saying, but honestly, I found people were very quick to judge me for (1) having sex and (2) "letting" myself get pregnant. As a young, married mom with three children, I still get people judging me. Don't place blame on her for her situation. Do your best to remain completely objective.

- *Share the success stories.* Counteract her doubt with the stories you know of inspirational young mothers— mothers who have made the mom, school, and job thing all work together. For some good examples, check out my website series, "Your Lines," which features interviews with some amazing young mothers.

- *Put things into perspective.* My mom did this for me, and I am eternally grateful. It's not a car wreck, it's not cancer. It's a baby!

- *Help her to get involved.* You know what helped me the most during my pregnancy? Connecting with other moms. When my college didn't have a support group for pregnant and parenting students, I started one. Meeting other young moms, hearing their stories, and sharing our struggles, tears, and most important, cookies, helped us all to heal and gave us strength to go on. Encourage her to reach out to other moms and work to pave the way for the future. See the section, "Thirteen Steps to Changing Your Campus" for ideas and tips on practical resources she can utilize, such as starting a website or placing pregnancy packets in her campus health center.

- *Point out the resources.* The hard thing about being a young mom is that we can all be too busy to talk about our experiences. From the best place on campus to breast-feed to answers about scholarships and kid-friendly places to study, getting through college as a pregnant student can be difficult to navigate. Fortunately, a lot of young moms and organizations work together on resources for pregnant students and young mothers (like this book, ahem). See a complete list of resources on page 133 to become familiar with help that is available.

  Example: "I know it can seem overwhelming right now, but I know moms like you who have done this. Have you heard of the blog *Mrs. Mommy, MD*? She was a senior in college at Michigan about to head to medical school when she found out she was pregnant. She didn't give up and is now in her medical school of choice, at the top of her class, all with her adorable two-year-old son. You should check her out!"

While this list is meant to guide you in best helping a woman facing a crisis pregnancy, please know that every woman will react to her pregnancy differently. There simply isn't a "right" or a "wrong" way to get through an unplanned pregnancy, just as there isn't always a "right" or a "wrong" thing to say to her.

I encourage you to follow her lead and to relax—the most important thing you can convey to her is that you do care about her. Trust yourself. Just as you will encourage her, please believe that you can do this! You are offering such valuable and lifesaving support to women and their babies, and I thank you for all that you are doing, whether it's offering prayers, volunteering at a crisis pregnancy center, or simply passing this book along to a young mom in need of encouragement.

Six Lessons
from an Unwed Mother

During my pregnancy, instead of daydreaming about holding my beautiful bundle of joy, I reflected on a few of the lessons that unwed motherhood had taught me.

Lesson 1: It's always the girl's fault.

I found out that getting pregnant is always the girls' fault—in the endless gossip that went on about me, it was whispered that I wasn't "strong enough to say no." Over coffee one morning, a coworker, well aware that I was pregnant, disgustedly told me she couldn't understand how in this day and age, with all the birth control options out there, anyone could be "stupid enough" to let herself get pregnant.

My bad.

I'm not sure where this one originates—I guess it's because girls are considered the moral gatekeepers or that people assume girls will be on birth control, but this one was frustrating to me. And although not everyone I know or have interviewed for this book became pregnant out of a relationship, it's not like we got pregnant by ourselves.

Lesson 2: All mothers are not created equal.

I learned this lesson on Christmas Eve, five days before my wedding, as I found myself standing next to an older, married woman of the community in the back of the church. She had a well-paying job, a loving husband, and had adopted a child after being told she could never have children. And she had just discovered she was pregnant. There we stood—two women with unplanned pregnancies. Person after person walked up to the woman and congratulated her on her "miracle from God," but do you think anyone congratulated me? (Hint: The answer is no.) When you are young, unmarried, and pregnant, people become confused—should they congratulate you or offer their condolences?

A baby doesn't exactly care how much money you have or if you've finished college—a baby just wants someone to love him or her. I think a lot of the trouble lies in moms trying to fight their motherhood, worried it's something "uncool," or too afraid that they won't do a good job to even try.

It's who we are right now. We are moms. But that doesn't mean we all have to wear the same mom jeans. Embrace your strengths as a young mom, but don't be afraid to admit that you are still learning.

Lesson 3: Skinny people multiply when you are pregnant.

I have no explanation for this lesson. All I know is that suddenly, the campus was teeming with women wearing skintight sweatpants with the word "Juicy" written across their butts. And of course, it goes without saying, but while the skinny people multiplied, so did my weight. Perhaps they could fit into those tiny sweatpants, but I had the ability to gain eight pounds in five days. Ha!

Lesson 4: It is possible to puke on an empty stomach.

That's all I'll say about that one. It is better that way, trust me. I am praying right now that you have managed to escape learning this particular lesson, because it really is no fun.

Lesson 5: I am stronger than I thought.

Lying in my bed one clear, cold night with the stars steady and bright through my window, I also realized the lesson that finally proved to me that I was ready to become a mother.

What I discovered about myself came as a surprise—a strength I didn't know existed. While the world may have seen me as an unlucky statistic, a person to be pitied, I learned to hold my head high and to be proud of my choice. Balancing my book bag and my baby belly, I faced a world that is still saddled with the false stereotype of a young, ignorant, unmarried mother.

Lesson 6: I had nothing to be afraid of.

And nine days after my twenty-second birthday, exactly one week after my college graduation, I learned my final lesson.

I will never forget—it happened on Saturday, May 17, at 4:51 p.m. It was a moment I feared so much; yet, it became laughable as I gazed down at the most beautiful sight in the entire world . . . my daughter.

Chaunie Marie Brusie is a writer, editor, speaker, obstetric nurse, and advocate for women facing unexpected pregnancy. In addition to serving as the assistant editor of the FAMILY Magazines of Michiana, Brusie contributes regularly to several parenting sites, including *Babble, Everyday Family,* and *SheKnows.* Her work has also been featured in national publications such as *Parents, American Baby,* and *Pregnancy and Newborn.*

Brusie began working in the pro-life movement long before experiencing her own unexpected pregnancy during her senior year of college, but from the moment those two tiny blue lines appeared for her, she realized that things look a little different on the other side. After discovering a startling lack of resources and support for student parents at her own campus and realizing that the majority of abortions occur in college-aged women, Brusie worked to equip her campus to better support mothers and student parents.

She went on not only to change her campus and help other student mothers, but also to graduate on time—with honors—exactly one week before delivering her first daughter, Ada Marie. Since that time, Brusie has dedicated herself to advocating for young mothers through her blog and speaking engagements. Her work has been featured on *Catholic TV* and *The Boston Pilot,* among others.

As a speaker with Feminists for Life of America, Brusie shared her message at schools and institutions across the nation, including on Capitol Hill. She received the National Association of Pro-Life Nurses Scholarship in 2008 and her website, *Tiny Blue Lines,* was a *Babble* Top 25 Bloggers' Pick for pregnancy blogs in 2013.

Brusie and her husband have three children and live in southern Michigan. Visit her online at tinybluelines.com.

Founded in 1865, Ave Maria Press,
a ministry of the Congregation of
Holy Cross, is a Catholic publishing
company that serves the spiritual and
formative needs of the Church and its
schools, institutions, and ministers;
Christian individuals and families; and
others seeking spiritual nourishment.

For a complete listing of titles from

Ave Maria Press

Sorin Books

Forest of Peace

Christian Classics

visit www.avemariapress.com

 ave maria press® / Notre Dame, IN 46556
A Ministry of the United States Province of Holy Cross